CON

THE PONY CLUB EVENTING OBJECTIVES

Eventing provides The Pony Club with a competition requiring courage, determination and all-round riding ability on the part of the rider and careful and systematic training of the horse.

Its object is to encourage a higher standard of riding throughout The Pony Club and to stimulate among the future generation a greater interest in riding as a sport and as a recreation.

Every eventuality cannot be provided for in these Rules, and where a rule is not covered, the British Eventing Rule Book should be consulted. In any unforeseen or exceptional circumstances or any other issue in connection with Pony Club Eventing it is the duty of the relevant officials to make a decision in a sporting spirit and to approach as nearly as possible the intention of these Rules. It is the competitors' responsibility to ensure that they are complying with the Rules of the competition.

Where a rule states District Commissioner, Centre Proprietor also applies, and where Branch is stated, Centre applies.

"As a Member of The Pony Club, I stand for the best in sportsmanship as well as in horsemanship.

I shall compete for the enjoyment of the game well played and take winning or losing in my stride, remembering that without good manners and good temper, sport loses its cause for being. I shall at all times treat my horse with due consideration."

RULES

These Rules are based on British Eventing's current rules for Affiliated Eventing, amended where applicable. The term 'horse' in these Rules covers ponies as well.

This Rule Book is a guide for Competitors. Organisers should refer to the Eventing Organisers' Handbook in conjunction with these rules.

NOTE: Rules that differ from those of 2022 or requiring special emphasis appear in bold type (as this note) and changes are side-lined.

Rulebook Version: 23.1.0

THE PONY CLUB EVENTING COMMITTEE

Chairman

- Patrick Campbell
  Email: eventingchairman@pcuk.org

Members

- Catie Baird
- Julie Campbell
- Harry Meade
- Nicky Morrison
- Christina Thompson
- Sarah Verney
- Robin Bower (Area Representative)
- Sue Cheape (Area Representative)
- Saskia Davies (coopted)
- Amy Veitch (coopted)

Sports Development Officer - eventing@pcuk.org

Health & Safety - safety@pcuk.org

The Pony Club
Lowlands Equestrian Centre, Old Warwick Road, Warwick, CV35 7AX
Telephone: 02476 698300
pcuk.org

All Rules are made by The Pony Club Volunteer Committees including consultation with others.

The Pony Club Office provides administrative support and any queries or questions relating to these rules must be directed to the Chairman of the relevant sport and copied to eventing@pcuk.org.

SECTION A - GENERAL RULES FOR ALL PONY CLUB EVENTING

1. EXPLANATION OF COMPETITION

EVENTING is a three-phase competition - Dressage, Show Jumping and Cross Country, each of which must be completed mounted. The Dressage Test will be ridden first, followed by Show Jumping and then Cross Country.

This order will be adhered to at all Levels. Pony Club Eventing is graded from PC70, PC80, PC90, PC100, **PC Chairman's Cup** and PC110. PC110 (Pony Club Open) is the equivalent of British Eventing's Novice standard, PC100 (Pony Club Intermediate) is BE100 and PC90 (Pony Club Novice) is BE90. Please refer to the following tables. All competitors in the same class must complete the three phases in the same order. Each horse must be ridden by the same rider throughout. A horse may only compete once on any given day.

2. LEVELS OF COMPETITION

(Metric Conversion Table – Appendix C)

The maximum dimensions at each Level must NOT be exceeded in either Show Jumping or Cross Country.

SHOW JUMPING	PC70	PC80	PC90	PC100	**PC Chairman's Cup**	PC110
Max length of course	350m	350m	450m	450m	450m	450m
Speed	300mpm	300mpm	325mpm	325mpm	325mpm	325mpm
Obstacles Max height	0.75m	0.85m	0.95m	1.05m	**1.10m**	1.15m
Max spread - highest point	0.65m	0.85m	1.05m	1.15m	1.15m	1.25m
Max spread – base	0.90m	1.15m	1.25m	1.35m	1.40m	1.50m

Note: Only one upright and one ascending spread obstacle may be included up to the maximum height. All other obstacles must be 0.05m below maximum height.

The limits on the height and spread of obstacles laid down in the rules must be observed with the greatest of care. However, if it should happen that a maximum dimension has been marginally exceeded as a result of the material used for construction and/or by the position of the obstacle on the ground, the maximum dimensions laid down will not be considered as having been exceeded, but the permitted tolerance is 5cms maximum in the ring or practice area.

COURSE DESIGN – SHOW JUMPING

PC70, 80 and 90: It is recommended that the first three obstacles should be inviting to allow horses to gain confidence. Neither water jumps nor water trays are permitted. The course must include only one double combination **(at PC70 a two-stride double) and no trebles.**

PC100 and PC Chairman's Cup: Neither water jumps, nor water trays are permitted. The course must include one double combination and may include a further double but not a treble. There should be one square parallel.

PC100, PC Chairman's Cup and PC110: It is recommended that a BS Course Builder's advice is sought on course plans.

PC Chairman's Cup Championship: At the Championships the show jumping will be held on the final day in reverse order of placings. There will be a trot up prior to the competition.

At all Levels: When the second or third element of a double or treble combination is a spread, the distances must be as for two non-jumping strides.

CROSS COUNTRY	PC70	PC80	PC90	PC100	PC Chairman's Challenge	PC110
Length of course	Up to 1,800m	1600m - 2,500m	1600m - 2,500m*	1800m - 2,800m*	1800m - 3,120m*	2400-3,120m*
Speed	435mpm	435mpm	450mpm	475mpm	475mpm	520mpm
Obstacles No. of Jumping efforts	Up to 25	16-25	18-25*	18-25*	20-27*	20-28*
Max height	0.70m	0.80m	0.90m	1.00m	**1.05m**	1.10m
With height and spread Max spread - highest point	0.75m	0.90m	1.00m	1.10m	1.20m	1.40m**
With height and spread Max spread - base	1.00m	1.25m	1.50m	1.80m	1.80m	2.10m
With spread only Max spread without height	0.90m	1.25m	1.50m	1.80m	2.20m	2.40m
Drop fences Max drop	0.80m	1.20m	1.30m	1.40m	1.40m	1.60m
Jump into and out of water Max depth of water	0.20m	0.20m	0.20m	0.20m	**0.30m**	0.30m

*At the Eventing Championships, the length of the course may be increased to 2,500-3,500m and the number of jumping efforts may be increased to 25-30.

**If building a new spread fence, it is recommended that the overall maximum spread does not exceed 1.25m

Below PC90, Organisers may reduce distances, speeds, heights and number of obstacles.

At PC70 and PC80 there will be no penalties for going too slowly, but reverse time penalties will be applied for going too fast – Rule 32 g).

3. SCORING AND CLASSIFICATION

The competition is scored on a penalty basis.

a. Individuals

The penalty points incurred by a competitor in each of the three phases are added together to give his final score for the whole competition, the competitor with the least points being the winner. A competitor disqualified or eliminated in one phase is eliminated from the whole competition.

b. Teams

Only the lowest three scores of each team are counted. These are added together to give the team's final score, the team with the least penalties being the winner. If fewer than three members of a team complete the competition there is no team score.

4. EQUALITY

If the total penalty score for the three phases gives equality of marks to two or more competitors, the classification is decided by the best Cross Country score, that is the competitor with the lowest total of jumping and/or time penalties. At PC80, PC90, PC100, PC Chairman's Cup and PC110, if there is still equality, the best will be the competitor whose Cross Country time is closest to the optimum time. If there is still equality the best show jumping score (including penalties at obstacles and time penalties) will be taken into consideration. If there is still equality the best Dressage score will decide. If the scores are still equal the result shall be a tie. If the total scores of two or more teams in a qualifying position for the Championships are equal, all teams concerned will qualify. If the scores are equal for an individual qualifying place at the Championships, all parties concerned shall qualify. At PC70, where the lowest total of cross-country jumping penalties is equal and there are no time penalties for going too fast, then the marks for Show Jumping and Dressage as outlined above, will be the deciding factor.

5. PROTESTS OR OBJECTIONS

Any query about a competitor's score must be made only at the Secretary's Office. No approach may be made to the Judge, Timekeeper, Fence Judge or Official concerned. Protests or objections must be made in writing and addressed to the Official Steward, or at the Championships to the Secretary. At Area Competitions and the Championships, only District Commissioners or their Appointed Representatives are entitled to lodge a protest or objection. Protests must be accompanied by a deposit of £10 at Branch Competitions and £50 at Area Competitions and the Championships, which is forfeit unless the Official Steward or, at the Championships, the Official Steward / Jury of Appeal, decides that there were good and reasonable grounds for it. Protests or objections must be made not later than half an hour after the incident that gave rise to them, or half an hour after the scores have been published. Objections to Dressage scores must be made not later than one hour after the scoresheets have been released.

At Branch competitions the Official Steward shall give his decision which shall be final. At Area Competitions and the Championships, if the decision of the Official Steward is not accepted then the Jury of Appeal, after investigation, shall give its decision and this decision shall be final.

Should a breach of eligibility subsequently be discovered, then the Eventing Committee may disqualify the offending team or individual.

If said individual was a Member of a qualifying team and their score contributed to the qualification the team will be disqualified unless the qualification holds up using the discard score.

Where scores are published during an event on a live scoring system, these are provisional until confirmed by the Official Steward as the final results. It is of the utmost importance that competitors check their dressage sheets and take every opportunity to read published results, provisional or final, as soon as possible after each phase.

6. JURY OF APPEAL

The following people constitute the Jury of Appeal:

a. The Official Steward or Assistant Official Steward

b. A Dressage Judge

c. The Chief Show Jumping Judge

d. The Cross Country Steward

e. Any member of The Pony Club Eventing Committee present.

The Official Steward may appoint a replacement for any member of the Jury if the need arises. Any three members from the above shall form a quorum.

At the Championships the Jury of Appeal shall consist of those members of The Pony Club Eventing Committee who are present, and three of whom shall form a quorum. At both the Area Competitions and the Championships at least three members of the Jury of Appeal must remain on the ground until half an hour after the scores have been published.

7. AGE AND HEIGHT OF HORSES

No horse under 5 years of age is eligible. A horse or pony shall be deemed to reach the age of 1 on the 1st of January next following the date on which it is foaled and shall be deemed to become a year older on each successive 1st January. There are no height restrictions.

8. DRESS

New equipment is not expected, but what is worn must be clean, neat, tidy and safe.

It is the competitors' responsibility to ensure that their dress is in accordance with the rules. Contravention may incur elimination. Apart from XC colours and silks, brightly coloured accessories must not be worn.

a. The following rules apply to ALL THREE PHASES:

i. Hats and Hair –

Hair: Must be tied back securely, in a safe manner to reduce the risk of hair being caught and to prevent scalp injuries.

It is mandatory for all Members to wear a protective helmet at all times when mounted with the chinstrap fastened and adjusted so as to prevent movement of the hat in the event of a fall. This rule defines the quality of manufacture that is required. Individual Sports may also have additional requirements with regard to colour and type of hat. It is strongly recommended that second-hand hats are not purchased.

The hat standards accepted are detailed in the table below:

Hat Standard	Safety Mark	Allowed at the following activities:
PAS 015 2011 with BSI Kitemark		All activities
VG1 with BSI Kitemark		All activities
Snell E2016 onwards with the official Snell label and number		All activities
ASTM-F1163 2004a onwards with the SEI mark	SEI	All activities
AS/NZS 3838, 2006 onwards	Australian Standard Certified Product	All activities

- For cross country riding (80cm and over) including Eventing, Tetrathlon, Horse Trials, Pony Racing (whether it be tests, rallies, competition or training) and Mounted Games competitions, a jockey skull cap must be worn with no fixed peak, peak type extensions or noticeable protuberances above the eyes or to the front, and should have an even round or elliptical shape with a smooth or slightly abrasive surface. Noticeable protuberances above the eyes or to the front not greater than 5mm, smooth and rounded in nature are permitted. A removable hat cover with a light flexible peak may be used if required.
- It is strongly recommended that a jockey skull cap is worn for cross country riding over lower fences (less than 80cm).
- No recording device is permitted (e.g. hat cameras) as they may have a negative effect on the performance of the hat in the event of a fall.
- The fit of the hat and the adjustment of the harness are as crucial as the quality. Members are advised to try several makes to find the best fit. The hat should not move on the head when the head is tipped forward. Most helmet manufacturers recommend you visit a qualified BETA fitter.
- Hats must be replaced after a severe impact as subsequent protection will be significantly reduced. Hats deteriorate with age and should be replaced after three to five years depending upon the amount of use.
- Hats must be worn at all times (including at prize-giving) when mounted with the chinstrap fastened and adjusted so as to prevent movement of the hat in the event of a fall.
- The Official Steward/Organiser may, at his discretion, eliminate a

competitor riding in the area of the competition without a hat or with the chinstrap unfastened or with a hat that does not comply with these standards.

Hat Checks and Tagging

The Pony Club and its Branches and Centres will appoint Officials, who are familiar with The Pony Club hat rule, to carry out hat checks and tag each hat that complies with the requirements set out in the hat rule with a **pink** Pony Club hat tag. Hats fitted with a **pink** Pony Club, British Eventing (BE) or British Riding Club (BRC) hat tag will not need to be checked on subsequent occasions. However, The Pony Club reserves the right to randomly spot check any hat regardless of whether it is already tagged.

Pony Club (**Pink**) hat tags are only available to purchase from The Pony Club Shop.

Tagging indicates that a hat meets the accepted standards. No check of the fit and condition of the hat is implied. It is considered to be the responsibility of the Member's parent(s)/guardian(s) to ensure that their child's hat complies with the required standards and is tagged before they go to any Pony Club event. They are also responsible for ensuring that the manufacturer's guidelines with regard to fit and replacement are followed.

ii. **Jackets (Dressage and Show Jumping only) –** A traditional style of riding jacket must be worn with a Pony Club Tie or hunting stock. It is permitted to wear a Pony Club stock with any jacket. Jackets may be removed during riding in, provided the competitor is wearing a shirt that at a minimum covers the shoulders. During hot weather the Judges may give permission for competitors to ride without jackets, but shirts must cover the shoulders. Shirts should be white or cream. Number bibs should be worn for all three phases. The metal membership badge should be worn on the left lapel of the jacket. **Tailcoats may be worn for the Dressage phase at the PC110 Championships.**

iii. **Gloves –** Gloves are compulsory for the Dressage phase and optional for Show Jumping and Cross Country.

iv. **Breeches –** Breeches or jodhpurs must be white, cream or beige. If worn, branding must be on the left leg and not be longer than 20cms or wider than 4cm.

v. **Footwear –** Only standard riding or jodhpur boots with a well-defined square cut heel may be worn. Plain black or brown half chaps may be worn with jodhpur boots of the same colour. Tassels and fringes are not allowed. No other footwear will be permitted, including wellington boots, yard boots, country boots, "muckers" or trainers. Boots with interlocking treads are not permitted, nor are the boots or treads individually.

Stirrups should be of the correct size to suit the rider's boots (see the Stirrup rule). Laces on boots must be taped for Mounted Games only.

vi. **Spurs –** Spurs may be worn at Rallies and other events. Any misuse of spurs will be reported to the DC/Centre Proprietor, Area Representative and Training Chairman. Any reported riders will be recorded and monitored.

Sharp spurs are not permitted. Only blunt spurs, without rowels or sharp edges, and spurs that have a smooth rotating ball on the shank may be worn. If the spurs are curved, the curve must be downwards, and the shank must point straight to the back and not exceed 4cm in length. The measurement is taken from the boot to the end of the shank.

vii. **Body Protector**

The Pony Club follows the British Equestrian Standards for Body Protectors.

The use of body protectors is compulsory for all Cross Country riding and Pony Racing in both training or competing. If a Body protector is worn for any Pony Club activity it must meet BETA 2009 Level 3 standard (purple label) or BETA 2018 Level 3 standard (blue and black label) – see right.

For general use, the responsibility for choosing body protectors and the decision as to their use must rest with Members and their parents. It is recommended that a rider's body protector should not be more than 2% of their body weight. When worn, body protectors must fit correctly, be comfortable and must not restrict movement. BETA recommends body protectors are

replaced at least every three to five years, after which the impact absorption properties of the foam may have started to decline.

BETA 2009 Level 3 (purple label) body protectors will continue to be accepted at Pony Club competitions until 31st December 2023, from 1st January 2024 only body protectors that meet BETA 2018 Level 3 standard (blue and black label) are to be used.

Riders who choose to use the Woof Wear Body Cage EXO must lodge a key with the Event Organiser when they collect their number.

Air Jackets

The Pony Club follows the British Equestrian Standards for Air Jackets.

If a rider chooses to wear an air jacket, it must only be used in addition to a normal body protector which meets the Body Protector Rule and Standards. In the event of a fall, the air jacket must be fully deflated or removed before continuing, after which, the conventional body protector will continue to give protection. Air jackets must not be worn under a jacket and number bibs should be fitted loosely or with elasticated fastenings over the air jacket. Sports have specific rules relating to falls in competition.

viii. **Medical Armbands –** It is the competitor's responsibility to wear a PC/BE medical armband during the cross-country phase if they have a medical condition that may impact on their care in the case of an emergency. Conditions that are relevant includes serious past injuries/surgery, chronic health problems such as diabetes, long term medications and allergies. If in doubt competitors should consult with their own treating physician. Cards must contain the competitor's details where indicated and must be worn on the competitor's arm or shoulder in such a way as to be visible at all times. It is not compulsory for competitors without any medical conditions to wear a medical armband.

ix. **Jewellery – the wearing of any sort of jewellery when handling or riding a horse/pony is not recommended and if done at any Pony Club activity, is done at the risk of the member/their parent/guardian. However, to stop any risk of injury, necklaces and bracelets (other than medical bracelets) must be removed, as must larger and more pendulous pieces of jewellery**

(including those attached to piercings) which create a risk of injury to the body part through which they are secured. For the avoidance of doubt a wristwatch, wedding ring, stock pin worn horizontally and/or a tie clip are permitted. It is recommended that stock pins are removed for cross country.

x. **Buttonholes** may not be worn.

xi. **Prize giving**

Competitors must be correctly dressed in their competition riding clothes (jackets etc) for prize-givings, either mounted or dismounted. Only Saddlery that falls within the rules of the competition will be allowed.

xii. **Collecting ring / Course walking**

Whilst dismounted in the collecting area, or course walking (both Show Jumping or Cross Country) Competitors must be tidily dressed but not necessarily in riding clothes. Competitors should however be dressed in their riding clothes when walking the show jumping course at the Championships after 9am on the day of competition.

b. **DRESSAGE only**

- **Whips** – A whip of any length may be carried at PC70, PC80, PC90, but no whips are allowed at PC100, **PC Chairman's Cup** and PC110.
- **Gloves** - Must be worn.

c. **SHOW JUMPING and CROSS-COUNTRY only**

- **Whips – A** whip, if carried, must be held in the hand by the handle with the handle at the top. The whip must be "padded".

  The maximum length of the "Whip" is 70cm and must be no less than 45cm.

  - The "Contact area", is considered to be 2/5's (two fifths) of the overall length of the "Whip" and must be covered with a "Pad".
  - There must be no "binding" within 17 centimetres of the end of the "Pad".
  - The "Pad" must be smooth, with no protrusion or raised surface, and be made of shock absorbing material throughout its circumference such that it gives a compression factor of at

least 6mm.

- There is to be no wording, advertising or personalisation of any kind on the "Pad".

Use of the whip:

At all times, the whip must only be used

- For a good reason, as an aid to encourage the horse forward or as a reprimand.
- At an appropriate time, namely when the horse is reluctant to go forward under normal aids of seat and legs or as a reprimand immediately after a horse has been disobedient.
- In the right place, namely down the shoulder or behind the leg but never overarm.
- With appropriate severity.
- No more than twice for any one incident.

Excessive use of the whip anywhere at the event will result in disqualification:

- Use of the whip to vent a competitor's anger is always excessive.
- Use of a whip which causes injury e.g., Broken skin or a weal, is always excessive.
- Use after elimination or retirement is always excessive.
- Use on a horse's head, neck etc. is always excessive.
- Using the whip from the ground after a rider fall or dismount is always excessive.
- If the rider's arm comes above the shoulder when using the whip, this is always excessive.

d. CROSS-COUNTRY only

- **Body Protectors** are compulsory for training and competing.
- **A self-tied stock** is strongly recommended.
- As a minimum shoulders must be covered while competing.

e. Electronic Devices

Electronic devices (i.e. headphones, mobile phones etc. enabling another person to communicate with the rider) are not allowed whilst the rider is competing.

No recording device is permitted (e.g., head / bridle cameras etc.)

Stopwatches may be worn at PC90, PC100, **PC Chairman's Cup** and PC110 Levels.

9. SADDLERY

New equipment is not expected, but what is worn must be clean, neat, tidy and safe.

It is the competitors' responsibility to ensure that their tack is in accordance with the rules and that they present themselves for inspection. Any competitor who presents to compete in the wrong saddlery/equipment will not be allowed to compete until they decide to re-present in the correct saddlery/equipment.

Any competitor who then changes their tack in any discipline after the Tack Inspection will be disqualified from the competition.

The Official Steward has absolute discretion to forbid the use of any bit, gadget, spur or boot which he considers cruel or misused.

Any misuse of a bit / bridle will be reported to the DC / Centre Proprietor, Area Representative and Training Chairman. Any reported riders will be recorded and monitored.

Any equipment not covered in these Rules must be referred at least two weeks in advance of the competition to The Pony Club Office to allow time for the Chairman of the Eventing Committee to be consulted. All tack must be correctly fitted. Disabled riders are welcome to apply to The Pony Club Office to use special equipment.

Any unusual decoration of the horse with unnatural things, such as ribbons, flowers, glitter etc. in the mane/tail or applied to the coat is forbidden. Red bows in the tail are permitted for horses that kick.

a. The following rules apply to ALL THREE PHASES:

i. **Bridles –** Plain black or brown bridles only may be used. For safety reasons, leather bridles are recommended. The Micklem Multibridle is permitted without bit clips.

ii. **Nosebands -** Must not incorporate chain.

iii. **Bits -** All synthetic bits must be black, brown or white.

iv. **Tongue Straps and Tongue Grids** are not allowed. Tongue guards are permitted for Show Jumping and Cross Country only.

v. **Reins –** Split reins, Ernest Dillon reins, Market Harboroughs and balancing, running, draw, check or bridge reins of any kind are forbidden. (A running, draw or check rein is one that is attached to the saddle, girth, martingale or breastplate on the horse.)

Grass and Balanced Support Reins

Grass reins and balanced support reins are permitted at Pony Club rallies and competitions jumping up to 50cm or in the Walk and Trot Test subject to the following:

- only those reins shown in diagrams 1 and 2 (and 5) are permitted.
- the reins must be fitted to allow and not restrict the normal head position of the pony. The rein length must be sufficient to allow the pony to stretch over a small fence
- reins may be leather or synthetic material, if synthetic then a break point of leather or other suitable material must be included

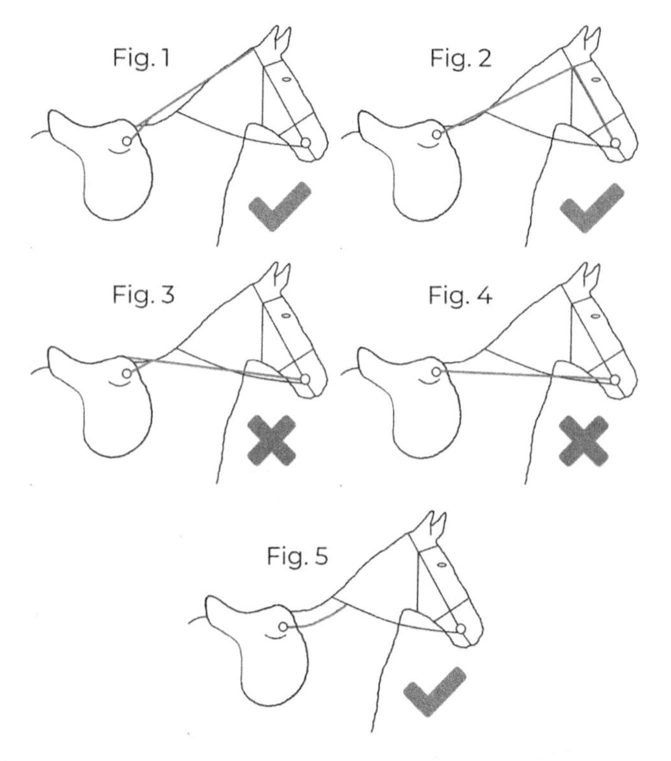

vi. **Neckstraps** may be worn in all phases at all levels.

vii. **Saddles –** Black or brown saddles of plain English type with white, brown, dark blue or black girths. Competitors wishing to ride side-saddle must notify the Organiser of the competition at the time of entry.

viii. **Stirrups** should be of the correct size to suit the rider's boots. They must have 7mm (¼") clearance on either side of the boot. To find this measurement, tack checkers should move the foot across to one side of the stirrup, with the widest part of the foot on the tread. From the side of the boot to the edge of the stirrup should not be less than 14mm.

There are now many types of stirrups marketed as 'safety stirrups'. All riders must ensure that their stirrups are suitable for the type of footwear they are wearing and the activities in which they are taking part and that the stirrup leathers are in good condition.

There are no prescribed weight limits on metal stirrups, however with the advent of stirrups of other materials, weight limits are frequently given by manufacturers. Any person buying these stirrups, should comply with weight limits defined on the box or attached information leaflets. Neither the feet nor the stirrup leathers or irons, may be attached to the girth, nor the feet attached to the stirrup irons.

It is strongly recommended that the design of the stirrup chosen allows the foot to be released easily in the event of a rider fall. Specific rules for individual sports can be found in the respective sports rulebooks.

Particular focus should be on ensuring that the boot and stirrup are the correct size for the rider taking part and used in line with the manufacturer's guidance.

For the avoidance of doubt, at Pony Club events:

- stirrups which connect the boot and the stirrup magnetically are not allowed
- Interlocking boot soles and stirrup treads are not allowed

ix. **Weighted Boots and pinch boots** are not allowed.

x. **Fly hoods, nose nets and ear covers –** are permitted for all competitions. The ear cover/fly fringe must not cover the horse's eyes. **Titanium masks are not permitted in Pony Club**

competitions except in Pony Club Show Jumping and the Show Jumping phase of Pony Club Eventing.

Ear plugs are not permitted and spot checks may be carried out.

Nose nets are permitted. Nose nets must cover the nose only leaving the mouth and bit visible.

xi. **Hoof Boots** – are not allowed.

xii. **Humane Girths** – are not allowed. Humane girths pose an increased risk as many common designs may have complete girth failure if a single strap was to break. Humane girths are not permitted in any Sport, whether during training or competition.

xiii. **Saddle Cloths/Numnahs** – Any solid colour is permitted. Contrasting piping is permitted. Branch logos are allowed when competing for the Branch; logos must not exceed 200 sq. cm. This does not preclude the wearing of clothing for horses or riders that has been presented by sponsors of the Championships in the current or previous years.

b. **DRESSAGE only**

i. **Bits must comply with current rules for British Dressage and must be used in their manufactured condition without any addition to/on any part. If in doubt, guidance should be sought from the BD Rule Book or by emailing The Pony Club office with a photo of the bit in question.**

ii. **Bit guards** are not allowed.

iii. **Nosebands** – One only of either cavesson, drop, flash, grackle or Mexican are permitted. Nosebands should be correctly fitted and should not cause discomfort. Nosebands must not incorporate chain or rope.

iv. **Martingales** and bearing, side, check or running reins are not permitted. Breastplates and cruppers are allowed.

v. **Boots and Bandages** may be worn whilst riding-in, but not during a Test.

vi. **Neckstraps** may be worn at all Levels.

vii. **Blinkers or cheek pieces** of any kind are forbidden.

c. **SHOW JUMPING and CROSS-COUNTRY only**

i. **Martingales –** The only martingales permitted are Irish, Standing, Running or Bib, only one of which may be worn at the same time. Standing martingales may be attached only to the cavesson portion of the noseband fitted above the bit.

ii. **Over girths –** Correctly fitted over girths are recommended for Cross Country riding with a double flapped saddle and a martingale/hunting breastplate.

iii. **Nosebands –** Only one may be worn unless using a standing martingale with a combination, Kineton or drop noseband or similar, in which case the addition of a cavesson is allowed. Nosebands should be correctly fitted and should not cause discomfort. Nosebands must not incorporate chain. Sheepskin nosebands are permitted.

iv. **Blinkers, leather cheek pieces** or any attachment to the horse or bridle which may affect the animal's field of vision are prohibited. Sheepskin **or leather** may be used on the cheek pieces of the bridle providing the sheepskin does not exceed 3cm in diameter measured from the animal's face.

v. **Bit guards** made entirely of rubber and smooth on both sides are permitted.

vi. **Tongue Guards** are permitted. The use of tongue straps, tongue grids, or the addition of string, twine or cord in or round the horse's mouth is forbidden.

vii. **In the Cross-Country and Show Jumping phases** any normal riding bit is accepted, hackamore or any bitless bridle. Bits should be in their original manufactured state.

10. ACTION AFTER A FALL

Any competitor who has a fall or sustains a serious injury anywhere at the competition site MUST see the medical personnel on the day and be passed fit to ride before riding that horse in a further test or before riding any other horse.

11. HEAD INJURY AND CONCUSSION

There are strict procedures around the response to concussion.

(i) General Advice

Head injuries and concussion can be life changing and fatal. Serious head injuries are usually obvious, but concussion can be very subtle. It may not be immediately apparent but should be taken very seriously.

Members may be asked not to ride by an Official (including a first aider) who believes they may have sustained concussion either at the time of injury or from a previous injury (which may not have been sustained whilst riding). Concussion is difficult to diagnose, and practitioners of all grades must err on the side of caution. Thus, any decision must be respected, and professional medical support is advised to avoid further harm. Ignoring an official's advice about concussion breaches the Pony Club's Code of Conduct.

(ii) Incidents that could cause head injuries or concussion

Any Member involved in an incident that could cause head injury or concussion at a Pony Club activity (for example, a fall from their horse/pony) should be assessed by the first aid provider in attendance.

Dependent on the level of first aid cover, the exact process of diagnosing will vary depending/based on whether the Member has suffered:

- No head injury/concussion
- Suspected head injury/concussion
- Confirmed head injury/concussion

The process for diagnosing each option is covered in more detail below.

An assessment may make it immediately obvious that there is no cause for concern. Reasonable care should be taken to ensure Members have not sustained a serious head injury or concussion.

(iii) Unconsciousness

If a Member is unconscious following an incident they should be treated as if they are suffering with a confirmed concussion and the steps in point vii should be followed.

(iv) Who can diagnose head injury or concussion?

Diagnosis of a head injury or concussion can be carried out by Trained First

Aiders, Qualified First Aiders or medical professionals officiating at a Pony Club activity. If there is any doubt as to the diagnosis, the Member should see the highest level of first aid cover that is present who should make the diagnosis. If a definite diagnosis is not possible then the Member should be referred to a hospital or a doctor off site for a professional diagnosis.

The member must not ride again until they have been seen by a doctor/ hospital.

(v) Actions to be taken in the event of a suspected head injury or suspected concussion diagnosis

If a diagnosis of a suspected head injury or concussion is made by a first aider, the parents/guardians should be advised to take the member to hospital.

Any Member who has been diagnosed with a suspected or confirmed head injury/concussion should not be left alone and must be returned to the care of their parents/guardians where appropriate.

If a Member has a suspected head injury/concussion at an activity/ competition, organisers should inform the DC/Proprietor to ensure that the rider follows these guidelines.

Once a diagnosis of suspected head injury or concussion is made by the first aid cover present at the activity, then that decision is final. If a Member is advised to see a doctor because of suspected head injury/concussion and the parents/guardians decide not to allow the member to be examined (either at the activity or in hospital), the Member will not be allowed to ride again on the day and should be treated as if they have sustained a confirmed head injury/concussion. Depending on the circumstances, the decision not to allow further examination may be considered a safeguarding issue.

Where a doctor subsequently certifies that a Member does not have or did not suffer a head injury/concussion, and provides evidence that they are satisfied the Member is well enough to resume riding activity, that Member will be treated as if they did not sustain a concussion. Officials will endeavour to assess members in a timely way; however, head injuries can evolve over time, which may lead an official or professional to perform a series of assessments. A Member may miss a phase or part of an event during the assessment process and the Sport Rules for missing that phase or part will apply.

(vi) Actions to be taken in the event of a confirmed head injury or confirmed concussion

In the event of a confirmed head injury or confirmed concussion diagnosis, the doctor will advise the Member not to ride or take part in any activity that potentially involves hard contact for three weeks. The member may be advised that they could request a review of any ongoing concussion problems by a doctor (with experience in assessing concussion) after 10 days. If that doctor is happy to certify that the Member is not suffering with a concussion, the Member may ride again. Evidence regarding this decision is required, e.g. in the form of a medical letter. If no evidence is provided, the Member should not take part in any Pony Club activity that involves horses/ponies, whether mounted or unmounted, for at least three weeks after the initial injury.

(vii) Actions to be taken in the event of a diagnosis of a confirmed or suspected head injuries/concussions outside of Pony Club activities

Ultimately, it is the parent/guardians' responsibility to make a decision about the welfare of their child.

If a Pony Club Official becomes aware that a member has sustained a suspected or confirmed head injury/concussion and has been advised not to take part in any potentially hard contact activities, the Member must not be allowed to take part in any Pony Club activities that involve horses/ponies, whether mounted or unmounted for three weeks, unless appropriate medical evidence of fitness to ride can be provided by parents/guardians dated at least 10 days after the initial injury.

Please see Appendix G for the Head Injury and Concussion Flowchart.

b. Incidents that could cause head injuries or concussion

Any member / rider who, at a Pony Club activity, suffers an incident that could cause head injury or concussion (for example, a fall from their horse / pony) should be assessed.

The person who does this assessment will depend on the first aid cover that is in place for that activity. Depending on the level of first aid cover then the exact process of diagnosing whether the member has suffered:

- No head injury / concussion
- A suspected head injury / concussion
- Confirmed head injury / concussion

Each option is talked through in more detail below.

From the assessment being carried out it may be immediately obvious that there is no cause for concern. In the course of Pony Club activities, The Pony Club is well aware that there are different kinds of falls and that assuming every fall leads to a head injury would be counterproductive to the aims of the organisation. We ask that reasonable care is taken to ensure members / riders have not sustained a serious head injury or concussion.

c. Unconsciousness

If a member / rider is unconscious following an incident they should be treated as if they are suffering with a confirmed concussion and the steps in point f. below should be followed.

d. Who can diagnose head injury or concussion?

Diagnosis of a head injury or concussion (both confirmed and suspected) can be carried out by any level of first aid cover officiating at a Pony Club activity. These could be a trained or qualified first aider (including a coach), a paramedic or a doctor. If there is any doubt as to the diagnosis the member / rider should see the highest level of first aid cover that is present and they should make the diagnosis. If the first aid cover at the activity cannot reach a definite diagnosis then they should refer the member / rider to a hospital or a doctor off site for them to make a diagnosis.

It would be more usual for a trained or qualified first aider to say they suspect a head injury or concussion than to diagnose it themselves. If they are the highest level of first aid cover available at the activity that will mean the member / rider has to go off site to have the diagnosis made by a doctor.

The member / rider should not ride again until they have been seen by a doctor. This may mean that the rider will miss part of an activity or competition.

e. Actions to be taken in the event of a suspected head injury or suspected concussion diagnosis

If a diagnosis of a suspected concussion or head injury is made by a first aider, they should advise the parents / guardians to take the member / rider to hospital.

Any member / rider who has been diagnosed with a suspected or confirmed head injury or concussion should not be left alone and must be returned to the care of their parents / guardians where appropriate.

Once a diagnosis of suspected head injury or concussion is made by the highest level of official first aid cover present at the activity, then that decision is final. No one may overrule that decision on the day if it is made in good faith. If a member / rider is advised to see a doctor because of suspected head injury or concussion and the parents / guardians decide not to allow the member to be examined (either at the activity or in hospital), the member will not be allowed to ride again on the day and will be treated as if they have sustained a confirmed head injury / concussion. Depending on the circumstances, the decision not to allow further examination may be considered a safeguarding issue.

Where a member / rider is diagnosed with a suspected concussion by a first aider or paramedic and that member / rider subsequently sees a doctor who is sure that they do not have a concussion and did not suffer a concussion and will provide evidence that they are satisfied that the member / rider is well, that member / rider will be treated as if they did not sustain a concussion.

f. Actions to be taken in the event of a confirmed head injury or confirmed concussion

In the event of a diagnosis of a confirmed head injury or confirmed concussion, the doctor will advise the member not to ride or take part in any activity that potentially involves hard contact for three weeks. They will advise the member that they could, after 10 days, ask a doctor, who is experienced in assessing concussion (including in children where appropriate), whether they have any concerns about any ongoing concussion problems. If that doctor is happy to certify that the member is not suffering with a concussion, the member may ride again, providing evidence regarding that decision is provided. If no evidence that such an assessment has been made, the member should not take part in any Pony Club riding activity and/or any unmounted activity that may involve any hard contact for at least three weeks after the initial injury.

g. Actions to be taken in the event of a diagnosis of a confirmed or suspected head injuries/ concussions outside of Pony Club activities

The Pony Club has no official way of automatically knowing about members who sustain a confirmed or suspected head injury / concussion outside of Pony Club activities. A concussion may be sustained outside Pony Club activities, for example at riding activities organised by other BEF member bodies or at school football / rugby / hockey matches. It is for parents / guardians ultimately to make a decision about the welfare of their child.

However, if a Pony Club official in charge of any Pony Club activity becomes aware that a member has sustained a suspected or confirmed head injury

/ concussion and has been advised not to take part in any potentially hard contact activities for three weeks, they should not allow the member to take part in any mounted activities and/or any unmounted activities that could potentially involve hard contact for three weeks, unless the member or their parents / guardians can produce appropriate medical evidence of fitness to ride dated at least 10 days after the initial injury,

SEE APPENDIX G FOR THE HEAD INJURY AND CONCUSSION FLOW CHART

12. MEDICAL SUSPENSION

If a Member has been suspended from taking part in any activity/ competition/sport for medical reasons, this suspension must apply to all Pony Club activities until such time as the Member is passed fit by a medical professional to take part. It is the Member's and parent/guardian's responsibility to ensure adherence to this rule.

Medical letters are required, following a suspension for medical reasons, to allow a Member to take part in any activity again. The letter should be issued by the either the hospital or specialist(s) involved in treating the injury, where appropriate.

13. UNSEEMLY BEHAVIOUR

Unseemly behaviour on the part of riders, parents, team officials or team supporters will be reported as soon as possible by the Official Steward to The Pony Club Office. Offenders may be penalised by disqualification of the Branch or Branches concerned for a period of up to three years. Any competitor who, in the opinion of the Official Steward, has been rude or aggressive towards any officials at a competition, or who has behaved in an aggressive or unfair manner to their horse, may be disqualified.

14. PERFORMANCE-ENHANCING DRUGS

All performance-enhancing drugs are strictly forbidden and The Pony Club supports 100% clean sport.

a. Equine - Controlled Medication

It is clearly essential for the welfare of a horse/pony that appropriate veterinary treatment is given if and when required, including appropriate medication. However, medication may mask an underlying health problem. Therefore, horses should not compete or take part in training activities when taking medication, if the combination of the medication and the activity may have a detrimental effect on the horse's welfare. Therapeutic Use Exemptions (TUE) should be confirmed in writing by a Vet.

b. Human

Performance-enhancing drugs are forbidden. The Pony Club supports the approach taken by the UK Anti-Doping Agency in providing clean sport. The Pony Club disciplinary procedures will be used where doping is suspected including reporting to the UK Anti-Doping Agency.

c. Testing

All competitors should be aware that random samples may be taken for testing from both themselves and/or their horse/pony. The protocol used will be that of the relevant adult discipline.

Competitors and their horses/ponies at national or international level may be subject to blood tests in line with the Sports Council Policy on illegal and prescribed substances. All young people competing at these levels should be aware of this.

Reporting

(i) Anyone who has reasonable grounds for suspecting that a Member is using or selling an illegal substance must report their concerns to the District Commissioner/Centre Proprietor as soon as practicable. If there is an immediate risk to the health, safety or welfare of one or more Members then the Police must be informed as soon as possible. The person reporting their concerns must ensure that any material evidence is retained

(ii) Upon receiving a report of suspected use or selling of an illegal substance, the District Commissioner/Centre Proprietor should carry out an immediate investigation of the incident and the circumstances in which it occurred, and then decide upon the appropriate action to be taken. This will include:

- Informing the Member's parents/guardians
- Informing The Pony Club Area Representative who in turn will inform The Pony Club Office
- Informing the Police
- Suspending the Member concerned while investigations are completed
- Awaiting the completion of Police investigations and actions

Disciplinary Action

The normal disciplinary procedure should be followed in cases relating to alcohol or drugs, which can be found in The Pony Club Handbook.

For more information, please refer to the Welfare of Horses and Ponies at

Pony Club Activities Policy, available on The Pony Club website.

15. DISQUALIFICATION

The Official Steward or Chief Judge may disqualify a competitor at any stage of the competition

a. for dangerous riding, or

b. if, in his opinion, the horse is lame, sick or exhausted, or

c. for misuse of whip, spur or bit, or ill-treatment of the horse, or

d. for any breach of the rules, or

e. for unseemly behaviour, including bad language.

Use of the whip

At all times, the whip must only be used:

- For a good reason, as an aid to encourage the horse forward or as a reprimand.
- At an appropriate time, namely when the horse is reluctant to go forward under normal aids of seat and legs or as a reprimand immediately after a horse has been disobedient.
- In the right place, namely down the shoulder or behind the leg but never overarm.
- With appropriate severity.
- No more than twice for any one incident.

Excessive use of the whip anywhere at the event will result in disqualification:

- Use of the whip to vent a competitor's anger is always excessive.
- Use of a whip which causes injury eg. Broken skin or a weal, is always excessive.
- Use after elimination or retirement is always excessive.
- Use on a horse's head, neck etc. is always excessive.
- Using the whip from the ground after a rider fall or dismount is always excessive.
- If the rider's arm comes above the shoulder when using the whip, this is always excessive.

16. COMPULSORY RETIREMENT

At PC90, PC100, **PC Chairman's Cup** and PC110 competitors incurring more than 24 jumping penalties in the Show Jumping phase will incur Compulsory Retirement and will not be allowed to go Cross Country, but competitors eliminated for technical reasons (starting before the bell, error of course etc) may do so at the discretion of the Official Steward. At PC70 and PC80, competitors may continue at the discretion of the Official Steward. An accumulation of four refusals on the Cross Country course at PC90, PC100 and PC110 incurs Elimination, but at PC70 and PC80, competitors may be allowed to continue their Cross Country round at the discretion of the Official Steward.

17. DIRECTIONS FROM OFFICIALS

Competitors and their supporters must, under penalty of elimination or disqualification, obey any order or direction given to them by any official and they must, in particular, be careful not to do anything liable to upset or hinder the undisturbed progress of the competition.

18. SPONSORSHIP

In the case of competitors and horses, no form of advertising, and this includes a sponsor's name, may appear on the competitor's or horse's clothing and equipment at any Pony Club competition, other than branding, which must be on the left leg of the rider's breeches and not be longer than 20 cms or wider than 4cm.

This does not preclude the wearing of clothing for horses or riders that has been presented by sponsors of the Championships in the current or previous years. Sponsors at Area Competitions must not be business competitors of the main sponsors of the discipline, and must be approved by The Pony Club Office.

Any advertising material that is used by sponsors, whether it be in the form of display banners or programme material, must be tasteful, and not inappropriate to the image of The Pony Club.

19. HEALTH & SAFETY

Organisers of this event have taken reasonable precautions to ensure the health and safety of everyone present. For these measures to be effective, everyone must take all reasonable precautions to avoid and prevent accidents occurring and must obey the instructions of the organisers and all the officials and stewards.

Legal Liability

Save for the death or personal injury caused by the negligence of the organisers, or anyone for whom they are in law responsible, neither the organisers of this event or The Pony Club nor any agent, employee or representative of these bodies, nor the landlord or his tenant, accepts any liability for any accident, loss, damage, injury or illness to horses, owners, riders, spectators, land, cars, their contents and accessories, or any other person or property whatsoever. Entries are only accepted on this basis.

20. LONE COMPETITORS

Competitors attending a competition on their own must inform the Secretary and provide Emergency Contact Details and location and details of their horsebox.

21. DESTRUCTION OF SEVERELY INJURED HORSES

If in the opinion of the Official Veterinary Surgeon a horse is so severely injured that on humanitarian grounds it ought to be destroyed, the following procedure will apply.

If the owner or his authorised representative is present, the Official Veterinary Surgeon will first obtain his agreement. If the owner or his representative is not available, the Official Steward, acting on the advice of the Official Veterinary Surgeon, may order the destruction of a horse.

NB: Owners should be aware that this Rule is slightly at variance with The Protection of Animals Act 1911 Section 11, which states that, in the absence of the owner, a Police Constable acting on the advice of a registered Veterinary Surgeon may order the destruction of a horse. This Rule is framed to avoid unnecessary suffering to a severely injured horse.

22. VACCINATION

A valid passport and vaccination record:

- must accompany the horse/pony to all events
- must be available for inspection by the event officials
- must be produced on request at any other time during the event

All ponies/horses must be compliant with the current Pony Club minimum vaccination requirements - please see the website for the current rule.

Note: Events that are held at other venues may be subject to additional specific rules. For example, any horse/pony entering a Licensed Racecourse Property must comply with the Vaccination requirements as set by the British Horseracing Authority. Similar restrictions apply in the cases of certain polo venues. If you are intending to compete under FEI Rules you will need to ensure you are compliant with those Rules.

23. ORDER OF STARTING

The order of starting shall be drawn after entries have been received. This order shall be maintained throughout each part of the competition. The timetable should be regarded as a guide only and competitors who are not ready to start any phase in their turn may be eliminated.

24. INTERVAL BETWEEN PHASES

No horse shall be required to start the next phase less than 30 minutes after completing the previous phase.

25. EXERCISE

a. Competitors may exercise their horses only in the areas provided. They must not exercise in the car or horsebox park or among spectators. They must not enter or practise in the Competition Dressage arenas, the Show Jumping arena or on the Cross Country course on penalty of elimination.

b. On the day of the competition, horses competing may be ridden only by their designated riders or, in exceptional circumstances and only with the permission of the Official Steward, by another member of the same team.

c. Lungeing of a horse is only permitted in areas designated by the organiser who may also prohibit it completely at their discretion. If allowed, lungeing may be carried out by either the rider or other persons. Lungeing of a horse and rider is prohibited.

d. Whether competing or not, whilst exercising any horse at a Pony Club competition it is permissible to use only the saddlery allowed under the Rules.

e. When riding-in, especially in restricted areas, riders should pass left hand to left hand; they should not pass so close as to upset another horse.

f. Tack adjustments should be made in a safe area without causing an obstruction.

g. Trainers and other pedestrians should endeavour to stand out of the way of competitors.

26. RAPPING

Rapping at or anywhere in the vicinity of the event is strictly prohibited. Definition of Rapping: Raising, throwing or moving a pole, stick, rope or other object against one or more of the legs of a horse while it is jumping an obstacle, so that the horse in either case is induced to raise such leg or legs higher in order to clear the obstacle.

27. STALLIONS

Stallions may only be ridden with the written permission of the District Commissioner and must wear identifying discs on their bridles in the interest of safety.

28. DRESSAGE

a. The Test

i. For Area Qualifiers and the Championships please refer to the table below.

Level	Area	Championships
PC70 Regional Championships	**Preliminary PC70 Test 2022**	**Preliminary PC70 Test 2022**
PC80 Regional Championships	Grassroots PC80 Test 2018	Grassroots PC80 Test 2018
PC90	PC90 Eventing Test 2013	PC90 Eventing Championship Test 2015
PC100	PC100 Eventing Test 2015	PC100 Eventing Championship Test 2013
PC Chairman's Cup	PC110 Eventing Test 2022	PC110 Eventing Championship Test 2015
PC110	PC110 Eventing Test 2022	PC110 Eventing Championship Test 2015

ii. Where competitions are running in conjunction with BE events the relevant BE dressage test may be used with permission from The Pony Club Eventing Chairman.

iii. For all Branch and local Events, The Pony Club Introduction to

Dressage Test 2019 or the Grassroots PC80 Test 2018 may also be used.

iv. The Pony Club Tests are all shown in Appendix D.

v. The arenas shall be either wholly or partly boarded at the discretion of the Organiser.

vi. The tests are to be ridden from memory. At PC80, PC90, PC100, PC Chairman's Cup and PC110, commanders are not allowed, but tests may be commanded at PC70. There are no time limits.

b. Execution of the Test

All movements must follow in the order laid down in the Test. In a movement that must be carried out at a certain point of the arena, it is at the moment when the rider's body is above this point that the movement must be executed. All tests should be ridden with both hands except where stated otherwise on the Test Sheet.

All trot work may be executed sitting or rising at the discretion of the rider.

c. Entering the arena

No horse either ridden or led may enter any arena, other than the practice arena, except when actually competing, on penalty of elimination. Competitors must not enter the arena until the Judge has sounded the horn, rung the bell or signified in some other way that he may start. Entering before the Judge's signal may lead to elimination. Should the construction of the arena make it impossible for the competitor to ride round the outside before the Judge's signal to enter is sounded, he may, on the instruction of the Organiser and/or Judge, ride inside the arena.

d. Salute

All riders must take the reins and whip, if carried, in one hand when saluting and drop the other hand down by the side and bow with their head only.

e. Dismounting and fall of Horse and/or Rider

If, after the rider has entered the arena, he dismounts without a reason acceptable to the Judges, no marks will be given for the movement.

In the case of a fall of horse and/or rider, the competitor will not be eliminated, but will be penalised by the effect of the fall on the execution of the movement concerned and in the collective marks. At Area and Championship level a fall of horse and/or rider in the arena will result in the competitor being eliminated from the competition.

If the fall of horse and/or rider occurs in the warm up arena the rider must be checked by the paramedic/doctor at the event before being allowed to continue. If the horse falls, the horse must be checked by a vet before being allowed to continue. If a vet is not present the horse must be checked by the Official Steward before being allowed to continue.

f. Resistance

- **i.** Any horse failing to enter the arena within 60 seconds of the bell being sounded will be eliminated.
- **ii.** Any horse refusing to continue the test for a period of 20 consecutive seconds during the course of a test will be eliminated.

g. Grinding of teeth and tail swishing

Grinding the teeth and swishing the tail are signs of nervousness, tenseness, or resistance on the part of the horse and can be taken into account by the Judges in their marks for the movements concerned, as well as in the appropriate collective mark at the end.

h. Assistance

- **i. The Voice** – The use of the voice is prohibited and will be penalised by the loss of two marks from those that would have been awarded for the movement in which this occurs.
- **ii. Outside** – Any outside assistance by voice, signs, etc., is considered as assistance to a rider or to his horse. A rider or horse receiving assistance will be eliminated.

i. Leaving the Arena

A horse is eliminated if, during a Test, it leaves the arena when the surround is 23cm (9") high or more. Where the surround is less than 23cm (9") and is marked by boards or similar, no marks shall be given for the movement when the horse places all four feet outside the arena. Where the arena is marked only by a line or intermittent boards, it is left to the discretion of the Judge(s) as to the marks deducted. Any horse leaving the arena not under control will be eliminated and, for this purpose, the Test begins when the horse enters at 'A' and finishes with the final halt. Competitors should leave the arena at a convenient place in free walk on a long rein.

j. Errors of Course or Test

When a competitor makes an 'error of course' (takes a wrong turn, omits a movement etc) the Judge warns him by sounding the bell. The Judge shows him, if necessary, the point at which he must take up the test again and the next movement to be executed, then leaves him to continue by himself. However, in some cases when, although the competitor makes an 'error of course', the sounding of the bell would unnecessarily impede the fluency of the performance, it is up to the Judge to decide whether or not to sound the bell. In fairness to the competitor, it is recommended that the bell should be rung when a movement is executed at the wrong marker if there is the possibility of a similar mistake when the movement is to be repeated on the other rein.

If the Judge for any reason does not realise that one or more movements have been omitted until the competitor has left the arena he must: -

- **i.** Adjust as necessary the position of his marks and comments on his sheet to accord with the movements actually performed.
- **ii.** Give to each of the movements not executed a mark equal to the average of the collective marks entered at the bottom of his sheet (averaged to the nearest whole number, 0.5 to be rounded up).
- **iii.** Record the penalty for error of course. When the rider makes an "error of the Test" (e.g. does not take the reins in one hand at the salute, etc) they must be penalised as for an "error of course". The Judge should put a star against the movement concerned and mark for an error at the bottom of the sheet.

k. Penalties for Error of Course or Test

Every "error of the course", whether the bell is sounded or not, must be penalised:

- **First Error**
  2 marks
- **Second Error**
  4 marks
- **Third Error**
  8 marks
- The points deducted are cumulative; after three errors of course 14 points are deducted.
- **Fourth Error**
  Elimination
- After the fourth error the competitor may continue his performance to the end, the marks being awarded in the ordinary way.

l. Riding the Wrong Test

A rider who starts the wrong test for the class may be allowed to restart the test (at the Judge's discretion) subject to time at the end of the class. They will be penalised for a first error of course.

m. Penalties for Contravening the Rules

Contravention of the rules will incur elimination. Under certain circumstances, instead of elimination, the following penalties may be deducted

- Entering the Dressage Arena with a whip (when not permitted): 6 Penalties per Judge.
  The Judge will stop the test and continue it after the whip has been discarded.
- Entering the Dressage Arena with Horse wearing Boots or Bandages: 6 Penalties per Judge.
  The Judge will stop the test and continue it after the boots and bandages have been removed.
- Minor breaches of the Dress Rules (not wearing gloves, horse wearing a tail bandage): 2 Penalties per Judge.
- Entering the Arena before the Judge's signal: 2 Penalties per Judge

n. Time

The approximate time given on each Test Sheet is for guidance only; there are no penalties for exceeding it.

o. Lameness

In the case of marked lameness, the Judge informs the rider that he is eliminated. There is no appeal against this decision. If there are any doubts as to the soundness of a horse, the competitor will be allowed to complete the test and any unevenness of pace will be severely penalised. The competitor will then be referred to the Official Steward.

p. Dressage Scoresheets

Dressage scoresheets may be handed out once the dressage penalties for all competitors in the class have been calculated. It is important that this is done in good time so that any errors can be rectified before prizegiving.

q. Scale of Marks

The scale of marks is as follows:

- 10 Excellent
- 9 Very good
- 8 Good
- 7 Fairly good
- 6 Satisfactory

- 5 Sufficient
- 4 Insufficient
- 3 Fairly bad
- 2 Bad
- 1 Very bad
- 0 Not executed*

* 'Not executed' means nothing that is required has been performed.

The marks 10 and 0 must be awarded where the performance warrants their use. Half marks are allowed.

r. Scoring

i. The Judge's 'good marks' (from 0 to 10) are added together, then penalties for any error are deducted to give a final total of good marks.

ii. The percentage of maximum possible good marks available is then calculated. This value is shown as the individual mark for that Judge. In order to convert the percentage into penalty points, it must be subtracted from 100 with the resulting figure being rounded to one decimal digit. The result is the score in penalty points for the test.

iii. When there is more than one Judge, the resulting totals are then averaged.

s. Dressage Judges

- At PC110 Area competitions Dressage Judges will be taken from Lists 1 – 5.
- At **PC Chairman's Cup** and PC100 Area Competitions Dressage Judges will be taken from Lists 1 – 6.
- At PC90, PC80 and PC70 (Regional) Area Competitions Dressage Judges will be taken from Lists 1 – 6, or may be British Eventing Accredited Trainers or riders who have competed at British Dressage Medium or BE Advanced/FEI******** levels and above, and who have had experience of judging at Pony Club. BD Trainee Judges are also acceptable at PC90, PC80 and **PC70** Regional level.

29. SHOW JUMPING

a. The Test

The test consists of one round of the course, judged under the Rules of The Pony Club Show Jumping, amended where applicable. There is no jump-off.

b. The Warm-Up

i. The Course Builder is responsible for ensuring that a minimum of one upright and one spread obstacle is provided in each practice area. If space allows, there should also be a cross pole.

These obstacles are intended for warming up purposes prior to competing. They are not to be used for prolonged schooling by competitors or others immediately before, during or after a competition.

ii. All elements of practice obstacles must be capable of being knocked down in the normal manner and must not be fixed, jammed or positioned in a manner which prevents or hinders them from falling. One pole only may be laid flat on the ground at the ground line vertically below the front edge of the first element of the obstacle or up to 1m (3' 3") in front and parallel to it on the take-off side. At least one end of any other pole or plank forming part of a practice obstacle must be supported by a standard cup or fitting. Sloping poles are permitted on straight obstacles and on the front element only of spread obstacles but the unsupported end of this sloping pole must rest at or in front of the ground line. False ground lines are not allowed. Alternate sloping top poles are not to be used.

iii. Safety Cups are compulsory for all Pony Club Jumping Competitions on the back rails of spread fences and middle and back rails of triple bars. This includes practice fences in the collecting ring. These cups must be in use at all times and must NOT be removed from the wing stands.

iv. Practice spread obstacles must not be jumped with a front pole higher than the rear pole.

v. No pole or obstacle of any kind is to be held by hand for a horse to jump.

vi. Practice obstacles are to be jumped in one direction only. The direction in which the obstacle is to be jumped must be indicated with red and white flags or by red and white supports. The red flag or support must always be passed on the rider's right-hand side and the white flag or support on his left.

vii. The height of practice obstacles must not exceed the maximum height of obstacles allowed by the Rules for the competition in progress.

Examples of practice showjumping fences that are not allowed

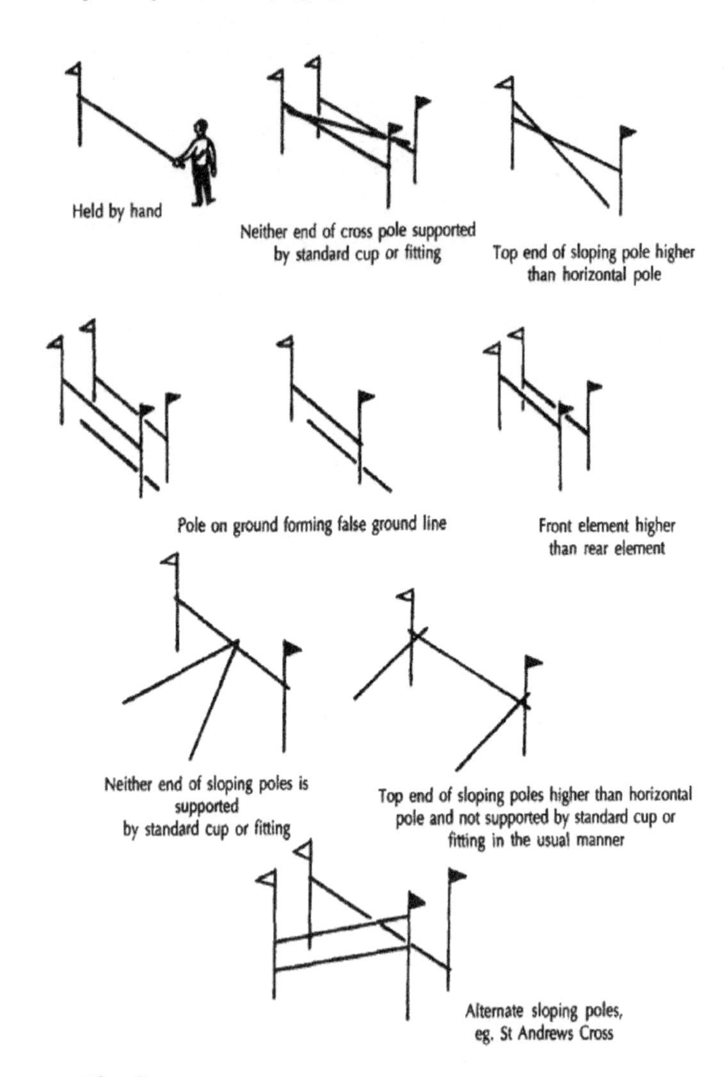

c. The Course

The course shall consist of not less than 7 nor more than 10 numbered obstacles, at least three of which shall be spreads. A combination must be included. The dimensions for the various Levels are given in the Table on page 5.

PC110 Area Competitions: A water tray may be included in one fence. There will not be an open water.

PC110 Championships: no obstacle shall exceed 1.15m in height or 1.25m spread at the highest point and 1.50m at the base except for a jump incorporating a water tray which must have at least two rails over it and may have up to 2.15m of spread. When the PC110 Championships is run in conjunction with a BE National or International Event there may be slight modification to both the Show Jumping and Cross Country dimensions and distances. Please see current BE/FEI Rules.

PC Chairman's Cup Championship: no obstacle shall exceed 1.10m in height or 1.15m in spread at the highest point and 1.40m at the base. The course will include one double and a further double or treble combination.

d. Safety Cups

Safety Cups are now compulsory for all Pony Club Jumping Competitions on the back rails of spread fences and middle and back rails of triple bars. This includes practice fences in the collecting ring. These cups must be in use at all times and must NOT be removed from the wing stands.

e. All plastic covered poles must have a wooden core to ensure that they are the same weight as a painted timber pole.

f. Penalties

- **Knocking down obstacle**
  4 penalties
- **First disobedience of horse**
  4 penalties
- **Second disobedience of horse in whole course**
  8 penalties
- **Third disobedience of horse in whole course**
  Elimination
  (Each circle or crossing tracks between fences counts as one disobedience)
- **First fall of rider**
  Elimination
- **Fall of Horse**
  Elimination
- **Error of course not rectified**
  Elimination
- **Failure to jump next fence within 60 seconds**
  Elimination
- **Failure to cross the finish line mounted**
  Elimination
- **Starting before the Bell**
  Elimination

- **Every commenced second in excess of Time Allowed**
  1 penalty
- **Exceeding the Time Limit (twice the Time Allowed)**
  Elimination
- **Exceeding 24 penalties (not including time)**
  Compulsory retirement

(Enforced at end of round)

At PC90, PC100, **PC Chairman's Cup** and PC110, competitors incurring more than 24 Show Jumping penalties will not be allowed to go Cross Country. Competitors at PC70 and PC80 may be allowed to do so only at the discretion of the Official Steward.

At all Levels, competitors eliminated for technical reasons (e.g., starting before the bell or an error of course) may be allowed to go Cross Country at the discretion of the Official Steward.

Time Penalties

When an obstacle is displaced as the result of a disobedience or fall: 6 seconds.

The bell is rung and the clock is stopped immediately, the rider may not continue until the bell is rung a second time. The clock is restarted at the moment when the horse takes off or attempts to take off at the obstacle where the refusal occurred. If a disobedience occurs at the second or subsequent part of a combination the clock is restarted when the horse takes off or attempts to take off at the first element of the combination.

Time penalties are added to the time taken to complete the round before the calculation of any time faults.

g. Timing

If the timing equipment permits, the 45 second count-down may be used according to BS Rules. It should however be explained over the public address before starting and at intervals during the first round.

h. Adjustment of Saddlery or Dress and Outside Assistance

Jumping or attempting to jump any obstacle or passing through the finish without a hat, or with the chin strap incorrectly fastened incurs elimination unless the Judge decides that the competitor was so far committed to jumping the obstacle at the moment when the chin strap came undone that he could not be expected to pull up before attempting the obstacle. In the case of adjustment to hat, chin strap, or saddlery becoming necessary during the round, for safety reasons outside assistance may be given. The clock will NOT be stopped and faults will be given as for a resistance (ceasing to go forward). If it becomes necessary for the rider to dismount, faults will be given as for a fall, ie. Elimination

i) Falls

- **i.** A horse is considered to have fallen when the shoulder and quarters on the same side touch the ground or touch the obstacle and the ground simultaneously.
- **ii.** A rider is considered to have fallen when there is separation between him and his horse that necessitates remounting or vaulting into the saddle.
- **iii.** If the fall of horse and/or rider occurs in the warm up area the rider must be checked by the paramedic/doctor at the event before being allowed to continue. If the horse falls, the horse must be checked by a vet before being allowed to continue. If a vet is not present the horse must be checked by the Official Steward before being allowed to continue.

j. Inspection of the Course

The course must be ready for inspection by competitors at least one hour before the commencement of the Show Jumping.

k. Plan of the Course

A plan of the course must be displayed by the time the course is ready for inspection, showing:

- **i.** The course to be followed and its length
- **ii.** The Time Allowed and the Time Limit.

l. Scoring

Any jumping and time penalties will be added together to give the competitor's penalty points for this phase.

30. CROSS COUNTRY

At PC70 Area level, if there is no cross-country course available, working pony or knock down cross-country fences (i.e., Jump4Joy) may be used provided they are in an open field/fields and not in an indoor/ outdoor arena or other confined space. There will be no penalties for any knock down fences.

a. The Course

The length of the course and number of jumping efforts will vary according to the Level. Please refer to the Table on page 7 for further details.

b. Inspection of The Course

- **i.** All Branch and Area Competitions – The cross-country course must be completed and ready for inspection by competitors, on foot only, by 2pm on the day preceding the Cross Country Test.
- **ii.** The Championships – The Cross Country course will be ready for inspection by competitors, on foot only, by 2pm on the day preceding the Cross Country Test. The Cross Country course may be open before this time but competitors must be aware that alterations may still be made.
- **iii.** Unauthorised alteration to or tampering with obstacles, direction flags or stringing and foliage on the course is strictly forbidden and will be penalised by elimination.
- **iv.** Plan or Map of the Course - A plan of the course must be displayed by the time it is open for inspection. It must include:

  - The course to be followed and its length
  - The Time Allowed and the Time Limit
  - The numbering of the obstacles
  - Obstacles having 'L' or black line Alternatives
  - Any compulsory turning points
  - Any hazards

c. Modification of the Course

- **i.** Before the Test Starts – After the course is opened for inspection by competitors at 2pm on the day before the Cross Country Test, no alteration may be made, except that, where exceptional circumstances (such as heavy rain) make one or more obstacles unfair or dangerous, the Official Steward is authorised to reduce the severity of or to by-pass such obstacles. In such a case the Cross Country Steward and every competitor must be officially and personally informed of the proposed alteration before the start of the Test. An official may be stationed at the place where an alteration has been made, in order to warn the competitors.
- **ii.** During the Test – NO modification to the obstacles is allowed but, if it is necessary in the interests of safety to order an obstacle to be

by-passed during the competition, all jumping faults previously incurred at that obstacle shall be cancelled with the exception of eliminations. A time allowance may be made at the discretion of the Official Steward. A competitor who has been eliminated shall NOT be re-instated in the competition. Once taken out, the obstacle shall NOT be re-introduced.

d. Marking the Course

Boundary Flags – Red and white boundary flags or indicators are used to mark the start and finish and compulsory sections of the course, to define obstacles and to indicate compulsory changes of direction. They are placed in such a way that a rider must leave a red flag on his right and a white flag on his left. Such red or white flags or indicators must be respected, under penalty of elimination, wherever they may occur on the course, whether singly or in pairs. Only obstacles which are numbered and marked by two boundary flags are judged as obstacles. All boundary and turning flags must be in position prior to 2pm on the day preceding the Cross Country phase.

All fences immediately adjacent to those that are included in the course should be crossed flagged to ensure the safety of Members and Spectators.

Direction Markers (Yellow or Orange) are placed so as to mark the route and help the rider in keeping to the course. They may be passed on either side and keeping close to them is not necessary. Boundary flags and direction markers shall be large and placed in conspicuous positions. Compulsory Turning Flags may be used only if absolutely necessary and will have the Red Flag on the right and the White on the left. They should be marked on the Plan of the Course.

Black Line Flags (a black line on red and white boundary flags) are used to show that an obstacle, either single or made up of several elements, has an alternative route which may be jumped without penalty. Both sets of flags will be marked with a black line. A competitor is permitted to change without penalty from one black line flagged route to another (e.g. jumping 9A left hand route then 9B right hand route) provided he has not presented his horse at the next element of the original line. After having negotiated all other elements, passing around the last element to be jumped will not be penalised.

The use of 'L' fence alternatives at PC110 is not encouraged at Area Competitions and the Championships, with instead more appropriate use of Black Flag / Long Route alternatives. Black flag alternatives should be sufficient in length to affect the time. **At PC70, PC80 and PC90 level "L" fences can be used to ensure that the course is of sufficient standard**

as an Area/Championship Test, while enabling the less experienced to complete their rounds. "L" fences may also be used at PC100 and PC Chairman's Cup level.

'L' markers are used to denote an easier alternative to the 'Main' obstacle, to help the less experienced to complete the Cross Country phase. All 'L' obstacles will be marked with red and white boundary flags and with a marker having a red 'L' on a white background beneath the fence number. Jumping an 'L' fence incurs 15 penalties. See rule 32 p) Alternative 'L' Obstacles.

e. Starting

At Area Competitions and the Championships, competitors must start from within a simple enclosure erected at the start and made of wooden posts and wooden or plastic rails measuring approximately 5m (16ft) square, with an open front marked with a red and a white flag. If this enclosure has an entrance at the side, this must be approximately 2m wide and should be padded or constructed in such a way that neither horse nor rider entering through the side can be injured. At Branch events red and white boundary flags on their own may be used at the discretion of the Organiser. A competitor may only start when given the signal to do so by the starter. The starter will count down from five before giving the signal to start and the competitor may move around the enclosure as he pleases. A competitor who starts early will have his time recorded from the moment he starts. Deliberately starting early or cantering through the start may incur elimination at the discretion of the Official Steward. If the horse fails to cross the start line within 2 minutes of the signal being given, the competitor is eliminated. Assistance within the starting enclosure is permitted, provided it ceases immediately the signal to start is given. From that instant, the competitor is considered to be on the course and any subsequent assistance is forbidden.

If a horse is lead into the start box the handler must wear protective headgear and gloves. Slip leads should be used, not metal clips.

f. Timekeeping

Time is counted from the signal to start until the instant when the horse's nose passes the finishing post. It is counted in whole seconds, fractions being taken to the next second above, e.g. 30.2secs. is recorded as 31secs. When it is necessary for an official to stop a competitor on the course while an obstacle is being repaired or because of an accident, the period during which a competitor is held up will be recorded by the Fence Judge and deducted from his overall time to give his correct time for completing the course.

g. Speed and Pace

Throughout the event, competitors are free to choose the pace at which they ride. They should, however, always take account of the requirements of each phase, the prevailing conditions and terrain, the fitness and ability of themselves and their horse and all other factors which may be relevant to the welfare of both Horse and rider. On the cross country course, they must also have regard to and respect the class speed, the optimum and 'too fast' times.

Deliberately slowing down near the end of the course to avoid time penalties is likely to incur a disciplinary sanction. **This includes slowing to a trot or weaving before the finish.**

At PC90 the Optimum Time for completing the course is calculated on a speed of 450mpm, at PC100 and **PC Chairman's Cup** it is calculated on a speed of 475mpm, at PC110 it is 520mpm. Exceeding the Optimum Time in PC90, PC100, **PC Chairman's Cup** and PC110 incurs 0.4 penalty points for every commenced second over the Optimum Time up to the Time Limit, which is twice the Optimum Time.

At PC70 and PC80 competitions an Optimum Time based on a speed of 435mpm will be used. No time penalties will be awarded for going too slowly.

Penalties will also be awarded in each case for going too fast. At all levels (PC70, PC80, PC90, PC100, **PC Chairman's Cup** and PC110) completing the course in more than 15 seconds under the Optimum Time incurs 0.4 penalties for every second commenced.

h. Penalties

- **First refusal, run out or circle of horse at obstacle**
  20 penalties
- **Second refusal, run out or circle at same obstacle**
  40 penalties
- **Third refusal, run out or circle at same obstacle**
  Elimination
- **Jumping the Alternative 'L' Obstacle**
  15 penalties

(The above penalty points are cumulative)

- **Four refusals around the course***
  Elimination
- **In PC110 three refusals around the course**
  Elimination

- **Fall of horse**
  Elimination
- **Fall of rider anywhere on the course**
  Elimination
- **Error of Course not rectified**
  Elimination
- **Omission of obstacle or boundary flag**
  Elimination
- **Horse trapped in obstacle**
  Elimination
- **Jumping obstacle in wrong order**
  Elimination
- **Re-taking, in whatever direction, an obstacle already jumped**
  Elimination
- **Jumping fence marked with crossed flags**
  Elimination
- **Horse resisting rider for 2 consecutive minutes anywhere on the course, including after being given the signal to start**
  Elimination
- **Every commenced period of 1 sec in excess of the Optimum Time (PC90, PC100, PC Chairman's Cup and PC 110)**
  0.4 penalties
- **For every second in excess of 15 seconds under the Optimum Time (PC70, PC80, PC90, PC100, PC Chairman's Cup and PC 110)**
  0.4 penalties
- **Exceeding the Time Limit (twice the Optimum Time)**
  Elimination
- **Deliberately slowing down near the end of the course**
  5 penalties
- **Continuing the course without a hat, or with chinstrap undone**
  Elimination

A competitor who deliberately starts before the Starter's signal or who canters through the Start will be subject to Discretionary Elimination by the Official Steward.

*Competitors at PC70 and PC80 only may sometimes be allowed to continue after the fourth cumulative refusal at the discretion of the Official Steward.

PC70 and PC80 competitors receive no time penalties for being too slow. Competitors will be eliminated for exceeding the time limit of the course.

i. Definition of Faults

Faults (refusals, run-outs, circling and falls) will be penalised only if, in the opinion of the Fence Judge concerned, they are connected with the negotiation or attempted negotiation of a numbered or lettered obstacle. Penalties incurred at an obstacle are cumulative (i.e. two refusals incurs 20 + 40 = 60 penalties).

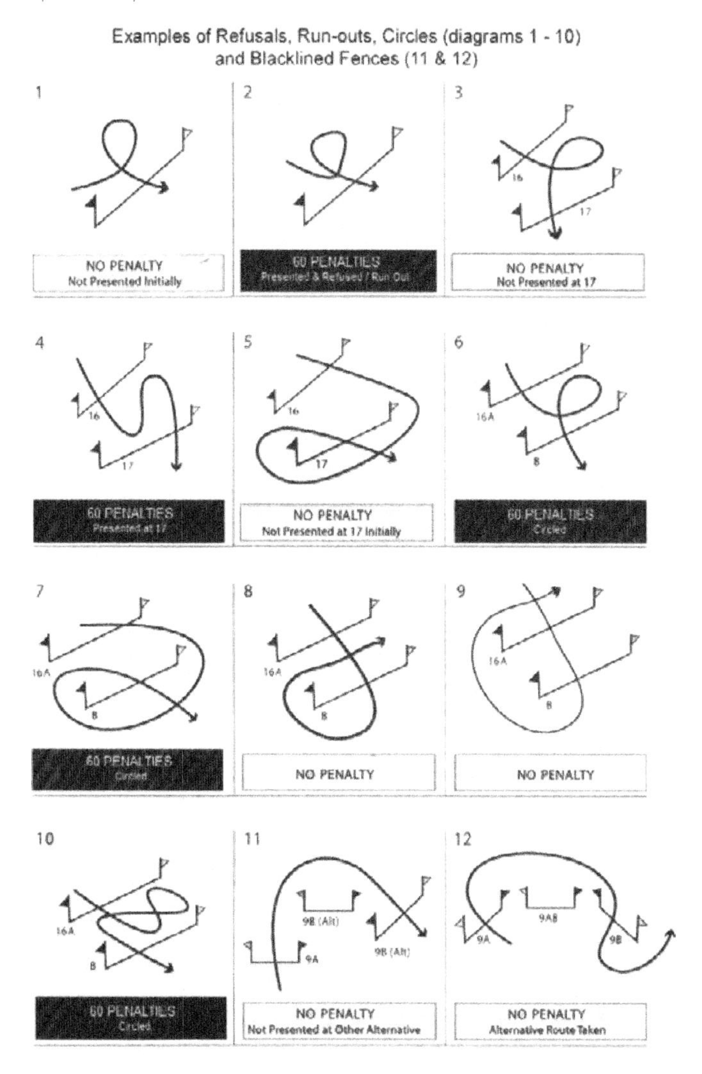

i. **Refusal** – At obstacles or elements exceeding 30cms in height: A horse is considered to have refused if it stops in front of the obstacle or element to be jumped. If a horse then jumps from a standstill this is considered a refusal and incurs 20 penalties. After a refusal, if the competitor redoubles or changes his efforts without success, or if the horse is re-presented at the obstacle and stops or steps back again, this is a second refusal (40 penalties). A third refusal at the same obstacle incurs elimination.

ii. **Refusal –** At all other obstacles or elements less than 30cm in height:
A horse is considered to have refused if it stops in front of the obstacle or element to be jumped. A stop followed immediately by a standing jump is not penalised, but if the halt is sustained or in any way prolonged, this constitutes a refusal. The horse may step sideways but if he steps back with even one foot, this is a refusal. After a refusal, if the competitor redoubles or changes his efforts without success, or if the horse is re-presented at the obstacle after stepping back and stops or steps back again, this is a second refusal and so on.

iii. **Run-out –** A horse is considered to have run out if it avoids an obstacle to be jumped and runs out to one side or the other.
A horse will be considered to have cleared a fence when the head, neck and both shoulders of the horse pass between the extremities of the element or obstacle as flagged.

iv. **Circle –** A horse is considered to have circled if it crosses its original track from whichever direction while negotiating or attempting to negotiate the obstacle, or any part thereof. If after completing the negotiation of all elements of an obstacle, a horse's exit track from that obstacle crosses its approach track to that obstacle, the horse is not considered to have circled, and will not be penalised. If a horse completes a circle while being re-presented at the obstacle after a refusal, run-out or fall, it is penalised only for the refusal, run-out or fall. A competitor may circle without penalty between two separately numbered obstacles even if they are quite close together, provided he clearly does not present his horse in an attempt to negotiate the second obstacle after jumping the first. However, if two or more elements of an obstacle are lettered A, B or C, (i.e. are designed as one integral test) any circling between these elements will be penalised. Except, at an obstacle where any of the elements is black flagged, after having negotiated all other elements passing around the last element to be jumped will not be penalised.

v. **Fall of Rider –** A rider is considered to have fallen when he is separated from his horse in such a way as to necessitate remounting or vaulting into the saddle.

vi. **Fall of Horse –** A horse is considered to have fallen when the shoulder and quarters at the same time have touched either the ground or the obstacle and the ground, or when it is trapped in a fence in such a way that it is unable to proceed without assistance or is liable to injure itself.

vii. **Knocking down a fence flag** – There is no penalty for knocking down a fence (boundary) flag. But if in the process the horse's head and shoulders pass the wrong side of the flag, i.e. to the left of the white or to the right of the red, the competitor must retake the fence and shall be debited the penalties for the run-out(s). Competitors may ask if they have to re-take the fence, and the Fence Judge is obliged to tell them. This is not considered 'forbidden assistance'. Flags do not have to be replaced by Fence Judges, but riders may request that flags are replaced. The time will not be stopped for competitors during replacement of a flag.

viii. There is no penalty for jumping a fence not on the course but the penalty for jumping a fence marked with crossed flags is elimination.

ix. **Overtaking**

Any competitor who is about to be overtaken by a following competitor must quickly clear the way. Any competitor overtaking another competitor must do so only at a safe and suitable place. When the leading competitor is before an obstacle and about to be overtaken, he must follow the directions of the Fence Judge. When the leading competitor is committed to jumping an obstacle, the following competitor may only jump that obstacle in such a way that will cause no inconvenience or danger for either. The penalty for wilful obstruction of an overtaking competitor, or failure to follow the instructions of the Fence Judge, or causing danger to another competitor, is elimination at the discretion of the Official Steward.

j. Competitor in Difficulty at an Obstacle

A competitor in difficulty or likely to cause an obstruction must give way to the following horse by quickly moving away from the front of the obstacle. If, in attempting to negotiate an obstacle, a horse should be trapped in such a way that it is liable to injure itself or be unable to proceed without assistance, the competitor will be instructed to dismount and will be eliminated.

k. Stopping Competitors

If any part of an obstacle is obstructed by a competitor in difficulty, or if any obstacle has been dismantled to release a fallen horse, or if an obstacle has been broken and is not yet rebuilt, or in any other similar circumstances, any competitor approaching the jump, and any subsequent competitors, must be prepared to stop on the instructions of the Fence Judge, who will wave a flag at waist height in the path of the oncoming competitor. The time during which the competitor is stopped will be noted by the Fence Judge and will be deducted from the time taken to give his correct time for completing the course.

Failure to stop is penalised by disqualification at the discretion of the Official Steward.

l. Forbidden Assistance

Outside assistance is forbidden under penalty of elimination. Any intervention by a third party, whether solicited or not, with the object of facilitating the task of the competitor or of helping his horse, is considered forbidden assistance. If, in the opinion of the Official Steward, the assistance was unsolicited and the competitor gained no advantage then no penalty will apply.

In particular the following are forbidden:-

- **i.** to intentionally join another competitor and to continue the course in company with him.
- **ii.** to post friends at certain points to call directions or make signals in passing.
- **iii.** for anyone at an obstacle actively to encourage the horse or rider by any means whatsoever.
- **iv.** to be followed, preceded or accompanied on any part of the course by any other person
- **v.** to receive any information, by any means whatsoever, about the course before it is officially open to the competitors.
- **vi.** for a fence Judge or official to call back or assist a competitor by directions to rectify an error of course.

EXCEPTIONS: Whips, headgear or spectacles may be handed to a competitor without his dismounting. Fence Judges are allowed to call 1st Refusal, 2nd Refusal etc.

m. Elimination and Retiring

Competitors eliminated or retiring from any part of the Cross Country course for any reason whatsoever must leave the course at a walk and take every precaution to avoid disturbing other competitors. They may not jump any obstacles after elimination or retiring.

n. Obstacles

i. Obstacles must be solid, fixed and imposing. Where natural obstacles are used, they must be reinforced if necessary, so that they present, as far as possible, the same problem throughout the competition.

ii. Obstacles will be numbered and flagged and must be jumped in numerical and/or alphabetical order. For Area and Championship level courses number colours must be in line with BE (or EI) colours:

- PC70 – Green
- BE80/PC80 – Purple BE90/PC90 – Orange
- BE100/PC100, **PC Chairman's Cup** – Pink or for **PC Chairman's Cup** Black if adding additional elements to the PC100 course; Yellow may be used if no PC110 class.
- BE Novice/PC110 – Yellow

iii. Obstacles should be designed within the limits of the different Levels to prepare competitors for the Championships, using 'L' Fences or Black Line alternatives to avoid eliminating the less experienced.

All obstacles must be sited so that a vehicle can get to them to evacuate casualties.

iv. All portable fences must be securely fixed with appropriate fixings to ensure the fence cannot move if hit by a horse.

o. Dimensions

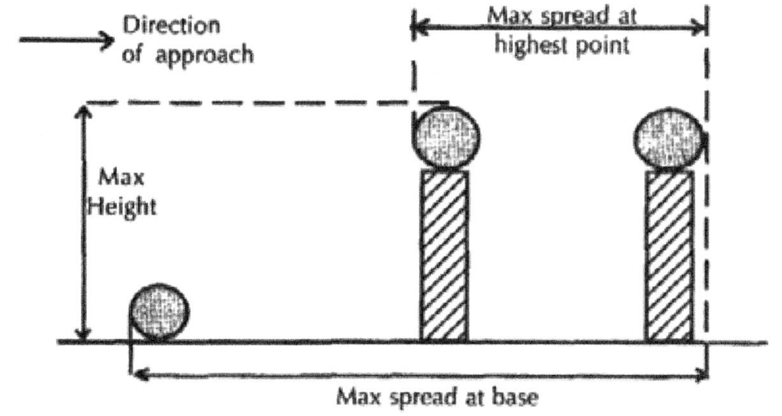

i. Obstacles are measured from the point from which the average horse would normally take off.

ii. When measuring the height of an obstacle it does not mean that obstacles must always be of uniform height or spread throughout their length, or that these dimensions may never be exceeded anywhere between the Red and White flags marking the extent of an obstacle. It is sufficient if that part of the obstacle, where the average horse and rider could reasonably and conveniently be expected to jump, does not exceed the maximum permitted dimensions.

iii. Obstacles with spread only (stream, ditch, etc) must not exceed the dimensions given in the Table on page 9. A low rail or hedge, provided that it merely facilitates the jumping of the obstacle is not considered to give height to this type of obstacle.

iv. Obstacles with both height and spread (oxer, open ditch, etc.) are measured both at the base from the outside of the relevant rails or other material making up the obstacle, and at the top from the outside of the relevant rails or other material making up the highest points (see diagram). The spread of an obstacle at its top is measured from both the outside of the relevant rails or other material making up the obstacle and the highest points.

v. In the case of an obstacle where the height cannot be clearly defined (natural hedge, brush fence) the measurement is taken to the fixed and solid part of the obstacle through which a horse cannot pass with impunity and which must be visible from the front. The overall height of a natural hedge or brush fence may not exceed the maximum height by more than 20cm.

vi. Poles used for timber obstacles must be not less than 10cm in diameter at their narrower end.

vii. In **PC Chairman's Cup** competitions it is permitted to add additional cross-country elements or fences to the PC100 course provided these abide by the dimensions given in Rule 2 (page 10).

p. Alternative 'L' Obstacles

The primary purpose of alternative 'L' Obstacles is to enable the course-builder to build a course at the right standard but which the less experienced competitor can complete. 'L' Signs are used as they are easily obtainable.

i. At Area Competitions and Branch Events 'L' obstacles will be provided as alternatives to some of the more difficult 'Main' obstacles and will be separate from them. 'L' fences and Black Line flags will be used at both Area Competitions and the Championships. See Rule 32 d) Marking the Course.

ii. An 'L' Obstacle may be an alternative to either a single or a multiple 'main' obstacle, but need not have the same number of elements.

iii. In a multiple obstacle, after jumping one or more elements of the 'Main' obstacle, a competitor may change to the 'L' element of the alternative obstacle that is next in sequence and vice versa.

iv. It is NOT necessary for a competitor to go back and jump any of the 'L' elements of an obstacle when he has already jumped the corresponding 'Main' elements, but he is at liberty to do so if he wishes in accordance with Rule 32 r) Combination Fences.

Marking

v. 'L' Obstacles and all 'L' Elements in a multiple obstacle will be marked with Red and White boundary flags, and with a marker having a red 'L' on a white background beneath the fence number.

vi. Each 'L' Obstacle will also be marked with the same number as the corresponding 'Main' obstacle. In the case of a multiple obstacle, each 'L' element will have the same letter as the corresponding element of the 'Main' obstacle. However, when the 'L' obstacle has fewer elements than the 'Main' obstacle, its last element will be marked with all the remaining corresponding letters.

Penalties

vii. Jumping (as opposed to attempting) an 'L' obstacle or any part of it will incur 15 penalties only (regardless of the number of elements) in addition to any penalties for Refusals, Falls, etc.

viii. Penalties incurred at the 'Main' obstacle and those at its alternative 'L' obstacle are cumulative. THREE refusals entail elimination.

q. Adjacent Obstacles

If two or more obstacles, although sited close together, are designed as separate problems, each will be numbered and judged independently. A competitor may circle between them without penalty, provided that this is not as a result of attempting to negotiate the next obstacle. He must not, under penalty of elimination, retake any obstacle that he has already jumped.

r. Combination Fences

If an obstacle is formed of several elements, each part will be flagged and marked with a different letter (A, B, C, etc) but only the first element will be numbered and all elements will be judged as one obstacle. They must be jumped in the correct sequence. A competitor who circles between two lettered elements incurs penalties. He may refuse, run out or circle only twice in all without incurring elimination. The third refusal within the obstacle as a whole eliminates. If a competitor refuses he is permitted to retake any elements already jumped, although he will be penalised for any new fault even if he has previously jumped an element successfully. They may pass the wrong way through the flags of any element without penalty in order to retake an element.

s. Banks on to the top of which a horse is intended to jump may not exceed the maximum height for the relevant Level given in the Table on Page 10. If the slope is sufficient to allow a horse to land on the face of it and scramble up, there is no limit to the height or spread.

t. **Bounces –** Double bounces are NOT allowed, except at steps. Single bounces, if included, must have an easier alternative that may or may not be an 'L'. If there is an alternative route, as opposed to an 'L' option, both sets of flags must be marked with a black line. (See rule 32 d).

Judging of bounce obstacles

At any obstacle where the distance between elements is 5 metres or less (i.e., a bounce) when a horse has negotiated the first element without penalty, it will be deemed to have been presented at the second element – and similarly if the bounce is for example the second and third elements of a combination. Thus, if a rider changes his mind while negotiating the first element of a bounce, and for example, then goes a longer route, he will still be penalised 20 penalties for a run-out.

u. **Bullfinches** are allowed, if it is possible to maintain them to the same standard throughout the day.

v. **Drops**

Drops should be measured from the highest point of the obstacle to where the average horse would normally land.

w. **Open Ditches** (i.e. ditches on the take-off side of the fence) must be clearly defined. If they have no guard rail they should be revetted on the take-off side.

x. **Water Obstacles**

- **i.** At PC 110, water obstacles which require a horse to jump over a fence into water may be included provided there is a black flag alternative obstacle ,and the underwater surface is sound.
- **ii.** At PC70, PC80, PC90, PC100 and **PC Chairman's Cup**, if there is no alternative, the entrance into the water must be a gradual slope

with no fence or vertical drop involved.

iii. In both cases the water must be at least 6m wide to ensure that a bold horse does not attempt to jump it and not deeper than 20cm for PC70, PC80, PC90, PC100 and **PC Chairman's Cup** and 30cm for PC110 measured at the point at which the average horse would land.. Likewise the water must not exceed this depth at the point where the average horse would take off. Elsewhere the water should not greatly exceed the maximum depth

iv. At PC90 **and PC100**, if there is a fence to be jumped in water an alternative should be provided

v. There should be no jump in the water at PC70 and PC80 level.

y. Hazards

Certain natural features such as ditches and 'drops' which, although not regarded as obstacles and therefore not numbered, might cause some horses to refuse may be classified as hazards. Their dimensions must not exceed the maximum allowed for other obstacles. Refusals, run-outs and circles and falls are not penalised at hazards. The only penalty is elimination if the horse resists its rider for 2 consecutive minutes.

Riders may not dismount and lead through or over a hazard on penalty of elimination.

z. Practice Fence

There will be a simple practice fence for warming up near the start, marked with red and white flags, which must be jumped with the red flag on the right. Only fences that are marked with red and white flags may be jumped in the warm-up area. Practice fences must not exceed the maximum dimensions allowed for the class.

aa. Scoring

The penalties incurred for faults at the obstacles and any time penalties for going too fast, or for exceeding the Optimum Time at PC90, PC100, **PC Chairman's Cup** and PC110, are added together to give the competitor's total penalty points for the Cross Country phase.

bb. Emergency Flags

Flags used by Fence Judges are as follows:

- Red – Doctor and Ambulance
- Blue – Veterinary Surgeon
- White – Fence Repair

- Orange – Course is blocked

Any flag being waved at waist height in the path of an oncoming competitor means that the competitor must stop.

NB The orange flag will only be used if a set of four British Eventing flags is available. If a set of Pony Club flags is being used, the Fence Judge will wave all three flags (red, white and blue) together towards Cross Country Control to indicate the course is blocked.

SECTION B – ADMINISTRATIVE RULES FOR AREA QUALIFYING COMPETITIONS AND THE CHAMPIONSHIPS

To be used in conjunction with all general rules. Some of these rules can also be used for Branch/Centre competitions.

Area Qualifying Competitions are to be held annually in each Area, from which those who qualify will go forward to compete at The Pony Club Eventing Championships. If an Area competition is over-subscribed, entries may be limited at the discretion of the Area Representative.

Where an Area has insufficient entries to enable it to run a PC110 Area Competition it may, with the agreement of The Pony Club and British Eventing, incorporate their Competition into a suitable British Eventing fixture. To comply with Rule 33 below this must be held in an "Open" Section(s) at the relevant level with no restriction on age of rider or grade of horse (other than those in Rule 33 below). Preparations must be made well in advance to enable arrangements to be made for those members who are not members of British Eventing, unregistered horses and/or those not complying with the current BE MER Rule for that level. (Organisers can obtain further details from The Pony Club Office re-entry procedure etc.).

An Area may also combine with another Area to run a joint competition. Please note that the new **PC Chairman's Cup** does NOT run under the same heights as the BE100+ so the Area Competition cannot be incorporated into a BE event.

Areas organising a PC110 Individual Area Competition may, if they wish, include a "friendly" inter-Branch team competition, but these teams will not qualify for the PC110 Championships.

Proprietors of Pony Club Centres may enter teams and individuals under the same rules as apply to Branch entries.

31. ELIGIBILITY FOR AREA COMPETITIONS AND THE CHAMPIONSHIPS

The District Commissioner or Centre Proprietor is required to certify the eligibility of horse and rider as follows. Should a breach of eligibility subsequently be discovered, then the Eventing Committee may disqualify the offending competitor.

Area – Members must fulfil all the following eligibility rules on the day of their Area Competition.

Championships – Between the Area Competition and the Championships, combinations who qualify for the Championships are permitted to compete in BE (or EI) competitions at a higher level than they are allowed to for the level at which they are qualified but not more than one level higher. Please see below.

PC110, PC Chairman's Cup, PC100, PC90, REGIONAL CHAMPIONSHIPS AND OPEN PC90

1. All horses graded British Eventing Advanced (Grade 1) (or Eventing Ireland Advanced) which have completed an AI/A level during the current year are ineligible at all levels.

2. All horses must be 5 years of age or over. A horse or pony shall be deemed to reach the age of 1 on the 1st January following the date on which it is foaled and shall be deemed to become a year older on each successive 1st of January. There is no height limit.

3. No horse may compete at more than one level of Eventing at Area or above (PC70, PC80, PC90, PC100, or PC110) in any one year nor may any horse be ridden more than once in any one year in any of the qualifying competitions or at the Eventing Championships. Combination of Horse and Rider cannot compete at two different levels of the same Sport at the Area Competitions. Except any combination of horse and rider may qualify and compete at both the PC110 Championship, and the **PC Chairman's Cup** Championships.

4. Stallions may only be ridden by Members if written permission is obtained from their District Commissioner/Centre Proprietor and they must wear identifying discs on their bridles in the interests of safety.

5. Riders or horses who have 'schooled' over the Area or Championship Cross Country courses during the previous two weeks are not eligible to compete. Competing over the course is permissible and does not render the competitor ineligible.

6. All competitors must be Members of The Pony Club both at the closing date for entries to the competition and at the date of the relevant competition to be eligible to compete at Area qualifying competitions and at the Championships (including the Regional Championships).

PC Chairman's Cup

This is a team and individual competition. At the Championships there will be a trot up prior to the Dressage Phase. The show jumping will take place on the final day in reverse order of placings.

In the event of over subscription, priority will be given to those who qualify at their Area competitions.

PC100

Area Competitions: Combination of Horse and Rider are NOT eligible if they have:

- **i.** Completed a PC110 or PC100+/Chairman's Cup Area Eventing competition or above in the current or previous years.
- **ii.** Completed a British Eventing (or EI) Intermediate or above.
- **iii.** Achieved more than three clear cross country rounds at British Eventing (or EI) Novice, (or Pony Trials, Open Novice or BE105.)
- **iv.** Previously ever finished 1st to 3rd as an individual at the Pony Club Eventing Championships on two occasions at PC100 level or above (this applies from 2021 onwards)

Championships: as for Area Competitions except that the combination of Horse and Rider are permitted to have:

- **i.** Completed more than three cross country rounds at British Eventing (or EI Novice, (or Pony Trials, Open Novice)

PC90

Area Competitions:

Riders are NOT eligible if they have:

- **i.** Completed a PC110 Area Level or above competition or British Eventing (or EI) Novice in Eventing in the current year or have done so in previous years.

Combination of Horse and Rider are NOT eligible if they have:

- **i.** Completed a British Eventing (or EI) Novice (or Pony Trial) or above.
- **ii.** **Achieved more than three cross country rounds with no jumping penalties at BE (or EI) 100.**
- **iii.** Achieved more than three clear cross country rounds at BE (or EI)100
- **iv.** Completed a PC100, PC100+/Chairman's Cup or PC110 Area level or

above competition in Eventing in the current year or have done so in previous years.

v. Previously ever finished 1st to 3rd as an individual at the Pony Club Eventing Championships on two occasions at PC90 level or above

Championships: as for Area Competitions except that the combination of Horse and Rider are permitted to have:

i. Completed more than three cross country rounds with no jumping penalties at BE (or EI) 100

OPEN PC90

1. Open to all Members who are not eligible for the PC90.

2. Eligibility is subject to points 1 – 9 at the beginning of this Rule.

This class is open to Individuals only.

PC80 REGIONAL CHAMPIONSHIPS

Area Competitions: PC80 Riders are NOT eligible if they have:

- Previously represented their Branch or Centre at PC90 or above in any Eventing Area Competitions.

Combination of Horse and Rider are NOT eligible if they have:

- Completed at PC90 or above Eventing at Area or Championship level, or BE90 (or EI) competition.

Championships: as for Area Competitions except that the combination of Horse and Rider are permitted to have:

- Completed at BE90 (or EI) competitions

PC70 REGIONAL CHAMPIONSHIPS

Members must be aged 13 and under on 1st January of the current year.

Area Competitions and Championships: Riders are NOT eligible if they have previously competed at any PC80 or above Area or Regional competition for Eventing.

PC70 PLUS REGIONAL CHAMPIONSHIPS

This is a class solely for individuals. There is no team competition.

Members must be aged 14 and over on 1st January of the current year.

Area Competitions and Championships: Riders are NOT eligible if they have previously represented their Branch/Centre at PC80 or above in any Eventing competitions.

32. PC110, PC CHAIRMAN'S CUP, PC100, PC90 AND REGIONAL AREA COMPETITIONS AND CHAMPIONSHIP QUALIFICATION

a. Number to Qualify - each Pony Club Area will organise a qualifying competition. Branches will compete within their own Areas.

Craddock rosettes will be awarded to members in PC100, **PC Chairman's Cup** and PC110 who complete a clear round show jumping and a cross country round with no jumping or time penalties at Area Competitions and Championships. The rosettes will be sent to Area organisers by The Pony Cub Office.

Team competitions are open to teams that must consist of three or four members from each Branch/Centre of The Pony Club.

If the individual qualifiers are also part of a qualifying team the individual qualifying place shall pass down the line.

Individual competitions are open to all competitors in the team competitions, whose scores are automatically counted for this competition. In addition, all Branches/Centres are entitled to enter extra individual Members regardless of the number of teams they enter.

There will be no extra invitations to the Championships.

All team members qualifying for the **PC Chairman's Cup**, PC100, PC90, PC80 and PC70 must have completed the Cross Country phase at the Area Competition. If a rider is technically eliminated in the Dressage or Show Jumping phases, they should be allowed to complete the competition with the approval of the Official Steward.

All individual qualifiers for the **PC Chairman's Cup**, PC100, PC90 and Regional Championships must have achieved a Cross Country round with no jumping penalties at the Area competition.

In the case of equality in qualifying for the Championships, all parties concerned shall qualify. (See Rule 4).

The following qualify for the Championships:

PC110

Teams

All entries will be put in their relevant PC Area squad and the top three scores at the competition will count and eligible for the team prizes..

If a Branch has three or four qualified members at the Championships, then a Branch team can be declared.

Individuals

Must have either:

- Been placed in the top 10% at any BE110 competition **or equivalent with results on ponyclubresults.co.uk or eventingscores.co.uk**; OR
- Obtained double clears (i.e., No jumping penalties on two occasions at any BE **or equivalent**, or PC110 (including Area) competitions; OR
- Been placed first at their **own** PC110 Area Competition in 2022 with no jumping penalties; OR
- Gained 4 Minimum Eligibility Requirement Points (MERs) Between 1st August 2021 and 31st July 2023, one of which must be in the current year.

A MER can be gained by completing a BE110 or PC110 Area Competition or PC110 competition with:

- No more than 45 Dressage penalty points
- A clear Cross-Country round with no more than 30 time penalties; AND
- A Show Jumping round with no more than 12 jumping penalties.

With the exception of a MER gained at a PC110 Area Competition, the MER must have been gained no later than 31st July 2023.

In the event of oversubscription, entries will be selected by the Eventing Committee with priority given to those with the best results in the current year.

PC100 & PC CHAIRMAN'S CHALLENGE

Teams

- Winning team qualifies automatically
- 2nd team qualifies if 5 or more teams compete

- 3rd team qualifies if 10 or more teams compete

Individuals

- The winner of each section qualifies automatically
- 2nd in section qualifies if **8** or more competed in that section
- 3rd in section qualifies if **12** or more competed in that section
- 4th in section qualifies if **16** or more competed in that section

All Qualifiers for the PC110 Championship automatically qualify for the Chairman's Cup.

Also, individuals may qualify if they have a minimum of 4 MERS;

A MER can be gained by completing a BE100 or above or a PC100 or above (with results on Ponyclubresults.co.uk or eventingscores.co.uk) with:

- **no more than 45 dressage penalty points;**
- **a clear round cross country with no more than 30-time penalties and**
- **a show jumping round with no more than 12 jumping penalties.**

MERS must be gained between 21st August 2022 and 31st July 2023.

Those members who qualify through the MERS route may be added to a Branch team to increase the number to four. They may not displace a member who qualified at their Area Competition unless that member is unable to compete.

In the event of oversubscription priority will be given to those who qualify via their Area competition.

PC90

Teams

- Winning team qualifies automatically
- 2nd team qualifies if **11 - 20** teams compete
- 3rd team qualifies if **21 - 28** teams compete
- 4th team if more than **28** teams compete

Individuals

- The winner of each section qualifies automatically

- **The 2nd qualifies if more than 12 competed in that section**
- **The 3rd qualifies if more than 16 competed in that section**
- **The 4th qualifies if more than 20 competed in that section**

OPEN PC90

Teams are not eligible.

Individuals

- If two sections are run the 1st place in each section qualifies.
- If one section is run 1st and 2nd places qualify.

PC80 (Regional Championships)

Teams

- Top 6 teams to qualify
- **The 7th team to qualify if more than 12 teams start.**

Individuals

- **If one section is run, the top 16 individuals will qualify.**
- **If two sections are run, the top 8 individuals in each section will qualify.**
- **If four sections are run, the top 4 individuals in each section will qualify.**

Places can be passed down in the member has already qualified in a team. **In addition, all individuals who have no jumping penalties cross country and no more than 4 faults show jumping will qualify.**

PC70 (Regional Championships)

Members must be aged 13 and under on 1st January of the current year.

Teams

- **Top four teams to qualify.**

Members of Qualifying Teams must not have more than 20 jumping penalties cross country. If a team is barred from qualifying as they do not have three members with fewer than 20 faults xc, those members who have achieved no jumping penalties cross country will be allowed

to compete as individuals. The team qualifying place will then be passed down.

Individuals

Provided that they have no jumping penalties cross-country:

- If one section is run, the top 8 individuals will qualify.
- If two sections are run, the top four individuals in each section will qualify.
- If four sections are run, the top two individuals will qualify.

PC70 PLUS (Regional Championships)

This is a class solely for individuals. Members must be aged 14 and over on 1st January of the current year.

Individuals

Provided that they have no jumping penalties cross-country:

- Top 5 individuals to qualify,

b. ELIGIBLE COMBINED TEAMS

Members from a Branch/Centre which has not entered a Team in the competition may be combined with Members from another Branch/Centre within their Area to form a Combined Team. This team must:

- consist of riders and ponies who would be eligible under these rules to compete in a Branch/Centre team.

- comprise three or four members from two Branches/Centres only, who cannot put forward a team of 3 or 4 themselves.

- contain no more than 2 members drawn from either Branch/Centre

- be entered by the closing date for entries and may only be created with the agreement of both the District Commissioners and/or Centre Proprietors concerned and the Area Representative.

- must have a named person with overall responsibility for the Combined Team identified by the District Commissioners and/or Centre Proprietors concerned.

Combined Teams, in order to be eligible to qualify for the

Championships, have to be pre-entered in the usual way, and not 'put together' after the close of entries.

If a Branch/Centre team is displaced from a qualifying place by an 'eligible' Combined Team, the next best placed Branch/Centre team wil also qualify

Combined Teams can only qualify for the PC Chairman's Cup if they have competed at their Area Competition.

Members from a Branch/Centre which has not entered a Team in the competition may be combined with Members from another Branch/ Centre within their Area to form a Combined Team. This team must:

- **consist of riders and ponies who would be eligible under these rules to compete in a Branch/ Centre team.**
- **comprise three or four members from two Branches/Centres only**
- **contain no more than 2 members drawn from either Branch/Centre**

c. AREA TEAMS

If a Branch/Centre has a Member(s) who is/are not included in a team, they may be put together with Members from other Branches/Centres in a similar situation to compete at the Area Competition. These teams can only be put together by the Area Representative and/or Area Organiser via a draw and all teams must be declared before the start of the competition or they will not count towards the number to qualify. They will be eligible to win rosettes/prizes at the Area Competition but cannot themselves qualify for the Championships

d. PC110 EVENTING AND PC CHAIRMAN'S CUP – TEAM AND INDIVIDUAL CHAMPIONSHIPS

Members are not required to qualify through the Area Competitions but ALL PC110 entries would have to be verified by the Branch DC/Centre Proprietor providing the members meets the criteria listed in rule 34a.

At the PC110 Championships, qualifying members will be put into their respective Area squad at the Championship and the top three scores from that squad will count. If a Branch has three or four qualified members at the Championships then a Branch team can be declared.

33. SECTIONS

a. Competitions should be run with four dressage arenas, A, B, C and

D. The first rider in each Team shall be judged in Arena A, the second in Arena B, the third in Arena C and the fourth in Arena D. Individuals can be placed into sections to even out numbers in each Arena and stagger the times of team members.

If it is possible to provide only two arenas for such a number of individuals, there shall be two sections in each arena, one after the other, with four dressage Judges.

b. If a competition has less than 72 competitors it is possible to run with only two Arenas, A and B. The first two riders of each team shall be judged in Arena A and the third and fourth in Arena B. Alternatively even numbered riders compete in Arena A and odd numbered riders in Arena B.

c. Where there are less than 20 competitors on the day it is permissible to run only one arena.

d. It is not permissible to run 3 Sections.

e. The Team Competition shall be judged as one with one winning team and one runner-up, etc.

34. ENTRIES – AREA COMPETITIONS

a. Entries must be submitted by District Commissioners on the official forms by the required date, together with the entry fee agreed by the Area Organiser to the Entries Secretary. A start fee may be charged if necessary.

b. If a Branch withdraws a team or individual before declaration, they must contact the Organiser for the refund policy.

35. ENTRIES – CHAMPIONSHIPS

Branches whose Team or Individuals have qualified for the Championships must declare their entries via the online entry system within seven days of completion of their Area Qualifier, or the following day if the Area Qualifier is held on or after the 31st July 2023.

PC110 competition will count towards a BE MER. Details for entries will be found on The Pony Club website.

There will be NO start fee charged.

Should a qualifying team / individual subsequently be unable to compete at the Championships, the next highest placed team / individual could be invited to compete, provided the substitution is made by 12 noon on

Monday 8th August 2022 and that, if it is an individual, a Cross Country round with no jumping penalties was achieved at the Area competition.

If a TEAM ceases to be eligible following withdrawals (fewer than three Members remaining), the team place would then be passed down the line, as long as the withdrawals are made by 12 noon on Monday 8th August 2022. The remaining individual/s from the team may retain their place/s.

District Commissioners are required to personally certify the eligibility of their riders and horses.

In addition to those qualified above, overseas Branches may be invited to compete, but at their own expense. They will be awarded appropriate rosettes but are not eligible for prizes in kind or bursaries.

36. WITHDRAWALS (ALL COMPETITIONS AND CHAMPIONSHIPS)

If a Branch or Centre withdraws a team or individual prior to the closing date for a competition, a full refund of entry and stabling fees will be made, less an administration charge. Withdrawals after the closing date for a competition will not be refunded.

37. ABANDONMENT (ALL COMPETITIONS AND CHAMPIONSHIPS)

In the event of a competition being abandoned, for whatever reason, a refund of 50% of the entry fee will be given. In such an instance the refund process will be communicated and must be followed.

38. SUBSTITUTION – AREA COMPETITIONS

After the closing date for declarations no substitutions may be made of horses or riders except in cases of illness, lameness or other unavoidable circumstances which must be certified by the District Commissioner or his Appointed Representative.

In such a case:

a. If a horse has to be substituted an alternative rider may be nominated.

b. If a rider has to be substituted an alternative horse may be nominated.

c. If a Branch enters more than one team a substitution may be made from one team to another.

d. No substitution shall be allowed after the Competition has started.

e. No horse or rider replaced by a substitute may re-enter the Competition.

f. In all cases of substitution the District Commissioner or his Appointed Representative must certify in writing that the substitute is eligible.

39. SUBSTITUTION – ALL CHAMPIONSHIPS (EXCEPT PC110)

a. Teams – the District Commissioner may substitute rider(s) and/or horse(s) in the Branch Team before entering. If a horse has to be substituted an alternative rider may be nominated. If a rider has to be substituted an alternative horse may be nominated. If a Branch has qualified more than one team, a substitution may be made from one team to another. The substitute rider(s) / horse(s) must have completed the Area competition.

b. If a team of three qualifies for the Championships, then a fourth team member may be entered at the Championships, as long as both the horse and rider are eligible and have completed the Area Competition.

c. Individuals – A substitute horse may be entered but not a substitute rider. The horse must have completed the Area Competition.

d. No substitutes shall be allowed after the Competition has started.

e. No horse or rider replaced by a substitute may re-enter the Competition.

f. In all cases of substitution the District Commissioner or his Appointed Representative must certify in writing that the substitute is eligible under Rule 33.

g. In exceptional circumstances and upon production of a Vets certificate a District Commissioner may request a horse substitution that falls outside the criteria detailed above. The Chairman of the Eventing Committee in consultation with the relevant Area Representative will consider the matter and their decision will be final. Any substitute horse must be qualified as per Rule 33, and horse and rider combination must have completed a ratifiable competition at the equivalent level during the current year.

40. BRANCH REPRESENTATIVE

If the District Commissioner of a competing team or individual is unable to be present at the Area Competition or Championships, they must inform the Organiser of the Competition, in writing, the name of the person appointed to be their representative. This should preferably not be either the Team trainer or parent of a competitor.

SECTION C – RULES AND GUIDELINES FOR ARENA EVENTING INCLUDING SPRING FESTIVALS

PONY CLUB ARENA EVENTNG

Arena Eventing is a two phase competition, which can be run on either an indoor arena, outdoor surface or a grass arena. General rules follow the current Pony Club Eventing Rule book except as modified below.

Competitors will jump a course of show jumps immediately followed by a course of cross country style fences**. There will be no more than 20 (dependent on size of arena) jumping efforts in total.

The optimum time should be based on a speed of 325 mpm (PC80 and below), and 375 mpm (PC90 and above).

Horses/Ponies must be aged 5 years old and over.

Stop Watches are not permitted.

The winner will be the competitor with the lowest number of penalties. In the event of a tie the winner will be the one closest to the optimum time.

There should be a drawn order and, where possible, approximate start times given in advance of the day

The course will only be open for walking before the class starts.

The Judge's decision is final.

PENALTIES

SJ Phase

- **Knocking down obstacle**
  4 penalties
- **First disobedience of horse**
  4 penalties
- **Second disobedience of horse in whole course**
  8 penalties
- **Third disobedience of horse in whole course**
  Elimination*
  (Each circle or crossing tracks between fences counts as one disobedience)

- **Fall of rider**
  Elimination*
- **Fall of Horse**
  Elimination*
- **Error of course not rectified**
  Elimination*
- **Failure to start or jump next fence within 60 seconds**
  Elimination*
- **Starting before the Bell**
  Elimination*
- **Continuing the course without a hat, or with chinstrap undone**
  Elimination*

*Competitors eliminated in this phase may not proceed to the XC phase

XC Phase

- **Knocking down an obstacle**
  4 penalties
- **First refusal, run-out or circle of horse at obstacle**
  20 penalties
- **Second refusal, run-out or circle at same obstacle**
  40 penalties
- **Third refusal, run-out or circle at same obstacle**
  Elimination
- **Four refusals around the course**
  Elimination
- **Fall of horse**
  Elimination
- **Fall of rider**
  Elimination
- **Error of Course not rectified**
  Elimination
- **Horse trapped in obstacle**
  Elimination
- **Horse resisting rider for 60 consecutive seconds anywhere on the course**
  Elimination
- **Failure to cross the finish line mounted**
  Elimination
- **Continuing the course without a hat, or with chinstrap undone**
  Elimination

Time will be taken overall.

- **Exceeding the time limit**
  Elimination
- **For every commenced second in excess of the optimum time**
  0.4 penalty
- **Every commenced second in excess of 5 seconds under the optimum time**
  0.4 penalty

Time limit is twice the optimum time.

NOTES

****XC Portable Fences/Fixed Fences** – These must not be used unless they can be properly and safely anchored. (See Eventing Organisers Handbook, and Guidance on Cross Country Fences. In their place, and especially on surfaces, knock down substitutes should be used, i.e. rustic show jumps or those supplied by specialist manufacturers such as "Jump for Joy"

If local conditions dictate, Organisers can choose not to time the Show Jumping Phase, but the XC phase must be timed.

Safety Cups – Safety Cups are mandatory for all Pony Club Show Jumping Competitions including any practice fences. To be used on the back rails of spread fences and middle and back rails of triple bars. They should also be used for all knock down fences in the XC Phase.

It is recommended a BS Course Designer, preferably one with Arena Eventing experience, is used if possible. For Area Competitions this is mandatory. If the course designer is not qualified, then approval must be sought from The Pony Club.

Courses should be built within the dimensions set out in the current Pony Club Eventing Rules.

First Aid – See The Pony Club Health and Safety Rule Book.

APPENDICES

APPENDIX A – METRIC CONVERSION TABLE

Metres	Feet/Inches	Metres	Feet/Inches	Metres	Feet/Inches
0.50	1' 7"	1.30	4' 3"	2.10	6' 10"
0.55	1' 9"	1.35	4' 5"	2.15	7' 0"
0.60	1' 11"	1.40	4' 7"	2.20	7' 2"
0.65	2' 1"	1.45	4' 9"	2.25	7' 4"
0.70	2' 3"	1.50	4' 11"	2.30	7' 6"
0.75	2' 5"	1.55	5' 1"	2.35	7' 8"
0.80	2' 7"	1.60	5' 3"	2.40	7' 10"
0.85	2' 9"	1.65	5' 5"	2.45	8' 0"
0.90	2' 11"	1.70	5' 7"	2.50	8' 2"
0.95	3' 1"	1.75	5' 9"	2.55	8' 4"
1.00	3' 3"	1.80	5' 11"	2.60	8' 6"
1.05	3' 5"	1.85	6' 1"	2.65	8' 8"
1.10	3' 7"	1.90	6' 3"	2.70	8' 10"
1.15	3' 9"	1.95	6' 5"	2.75	9' 0"
1.20	3' 11"	2.00	6' 6"	2.80	9' 2"
1.25	4' 1"	2.05	6' 8"	2.85	9' 4"

APPENDIX B - PONY CLUB DRESSAGE TESTS USED IN EVENTING

PC90 EVENTING TEST 2013

20mx40m Arena

1.	A C	Enter at working trot and proceed down the centre line without halting. Turn right.	10
2.	MB Btwn B & F MH	Working trot. Half circle right 15m diameter, returning to the track at M. Working trot.	10
3.	HXF	Change the rein on the diagonal, over X transition to walk 2-5 steps then return to working trot.	10
4.	FA A	Working trot. Medium walk.	10
5.	KXM	Change the rein in free walk on a long rein.	10x2
6.	M H	Medium walk. Working trot.	10
7.	Btwn E & K	Half circle left 15m diameter, returning to the track at H.	10
8.	Btwn C & M MB	Working canter. Working canter.	10
9.	B BF	Circle right 20 metres diameter. Working canter.	10
10.	Btwn F & A AK	Working trot. Working trot.	10
11.	KXM	Change the rein on the diagonal, over X transition to walk 2-5 steps then return to working trot.	10
12.	Btwn C & H HE	Working canter. Working canter.	10
13.	E EK	Circle left 20 metres diameter. Working canter.	10
14.	Btwn K & A AF	Working trot. Working trot.	10
15.	FX X	On the diagonal. Proceed on the centre line towards G.	10
16.	G	Halt. Immobility. Salute.	10

Leave arena at walk on a long rein at a convenient place.		
17.	Paces	10
18.	Impulsion	10x2
19.	Submission	10x2
20.	Rider position and seat	10x2
		240

All trot work may be executed 'sitting' or 'rising'.

Approximate time 4 1/2 minutes.

PC100 EVENTING TEST 2015

20mx40m Arena

1.	A	Enter at working trot and proceed down centre line without halting.	10
2.	C	Track right and immediately commence a 3 loop serpentine, with each loop going to the sides of the arena, finishing at A on the right rein.	10
3.	AKE E	Working trot. Turn right.	10
4.	X	Halt 3-5 seconds, proceed at medium walk.	10
5.	B BMC	Turn left. Medium walk.	10
6.	C HB	Proceed in free walk on a long rein. Change the rein in free walk on a long rein.	10x2
7.	B	Transition to medium walk and before F working trot.	10
8.	FAK K	Working trot. Transition to working canter right.	10
9.	E	Circle right 20 metres diameter. Give and retake the inside rein when crossing the centre line for the second time.	10
10.	EHCMB	Working canter.	10
11.	Btwn B & F	Transition to working trot.	10
12.	A	Half circle right 20 metres diameter to X.	10
13.	X	Half circle left 20 metres diameter to C.	10
14.	H	Transition to working canter left.	10
15.	E	Circle left 20 metres diameter. Give and retake the inside rein when crossing the centre line for the first time.	10
16.	EKAFB	Working canter.	10
17.	Btwn B & M MCHE	Transition to working trot. Working trot.	10
18.	E X G	Half circle left 10 metres diameter to X. Proceed on the centre line. Halt, immobility, salute.	10

Leave the arena at walk on a long rein at a convenient place.		
19.	Paces	10
20.	Impulsion	10x2
21.	Submission	10x2
22.	Rider position and seat	10x2
		260

All trot work to be executed 'sitting' or 'rising'.

Approximate time 4 1/2 minutes.

PC110 EVENTING TEST 2022

20mx40m Arena

1.	A C	Enter at working trot and proceed down the centre line without halting. Turn left.	10
2.	E B	Turn left. Turn right.	10
3.	A	3 loop serpentine each loop going to the long side of the arena and finishing on the right rein at C.	10
4.	MXK	Change the rein showing a few Medium Trot steps.	10
5.	A	Circle left 15m diameter in working trot.	10
6.	FXH	Change the rein and over X give and retake the reins.	10
7.	C	Circle right 15m diameter in working trot.	10
8.	Btwn C & M	Working canter right.	10
9.	B	Circle right 20m diameter.	10
10.	BFAK	Working canter.	10
11.	KXM	Change the rein and between X & M transition to working trot.	10
12.	Btwn C & H	Working canter left.	10
13.	E	Circle left 20m diameter in working canter.	10
14.	EKAF	Working canter.	10
15.	FXH	Change the rein with a transition to working trot over X.	10
16.	C	Medium walk.	10
17.	ME	Free walk on a long rein.	10x2
18.	EKA	Medium walk.	10
19.	A FX	Working trot. Working trot.	10
20.	X G	Continue on centre line. Halt and salute.	10
Leave the arena at free walk on a long rein at a convenient place.			
21.		Paces	10
22.		Impulsion	10x2
23.		Submission	10x2
24.		Rider position and seat	10x2
			280

All trot work to be executed 'sitting' or 'rising'.

Approximate time 5 minutes.

PC90 EVENTING CHAMPIONSHIP TEST 2015

20mx40m Arena

1.	A C	Enter in working trot and proceed down the centre line without halting. Track left.	10
2.	E EAB	Circle left 20m diameter. When crossing the centre line for the second time transition to walk for 2-5 steps proceed in working trot. Working trot	10
3.	B E	Turn left. Track right.	10
4.	B	Circle right 20m diameter. When crossing the line for the second time transition to walk for 2-5 steps proceed in working trot.	10
5.	Btwn F & A	Working canter right.	10
6.	E	Circle right 20m diameter.	10
7.	Btwn C & M	Working trot.	10
8.	MBAE	Working trot.	10
9.	E B	Turn right. Track left.	10
10.	Btwn M & C	Working canter left.	10
11.	E	Circle left 20m diameter.	10
12.	Btwn A & F	Working trot.	10
13.	Before B	Medium walk.	10
14.	B B	Circle left 20m diameter in free walk on a long rein. Medium walk.	10x2
15.	M	Working trot.	10
16.	E X	Half circle 10m diameter to X. Proceed down the centre line.	10
17.	G	Halt. Immobility. Salute.	10
Leave the arena at walk on a long rein at a convenient place.			
18.		Paces	10
19.		Impulsion	10x2
20.		Submission	10x2
21.		Rider position and seat	10x2
			250

All trot work to be executed 'sitting' or 'rising'.

Approximate time 4 1/2 minutes.

PC100 EVENTING CHAMPIONSHIP TEST 2013

20mx60m Arena

1.	A C CS	Enter in working trot and proceed down the centre line without halting. Turn left. Working trot.	10
2.	S SE	Circle left 15 metres diameter. Working trot.	10
3.	E B BP	Turn left. Turn right. Working trot.	10
4.	P PAV	Circle right 15 metres diameter. Working trot.	10
5.	VXR RC	Change the rein and show some medium trot steps. Working trot.	10
6.	Btwn C & H HS	Working canter. Working canter.	10
7.	S	Circle left 20 metres diameter.	10
8.	SV VAF	Show some medium canter strides. Working canter.	10
9.	FLE Btwn L & E ES	Change the rein on the diagonal. Transition to working trot. Working trot.	10
10.	Btwn S & H	Transition to walk 2-5 steps then return to working trot.	10
11.	Btwn C & M MR	Working canter. Working canter.	10
12.	R	Circle right 20 metres diameter.	10
13.	RP PAK	Show some medium canter strides. Working canter.	10
14.	KLB Btwn L & B BM	Change the rein on the diagonal. Transition to working trot. Working trot.	10
15.	M	Medium walk.	10
16.	HP	Change the rein free walk on a long rein.	10x2
17.	P F	Medium walk. Working trot.	10
18.	A X	Turn down the centre line. Halt. Immobility. Salute	10

Leave the arena at walk on a long rein at a convenient place.		
19.	Paces	10
20.	Impulsion	10x2
21.	Submission	10x2
22.	Rider position and seat	10x2
		260

All trot work may be executed 'sitting' or 'rising'.

Approximate time 5 minutes.

PC110 EVENTING CHAMPIONSHIP TEST 2015

20mx60m Arena

1.	A C	Enter at working trot. Proceed down the centre line without halting. Turn left.	10
2.	S	Circle left 15 metres diameter.	10
3.	SF F	Change the rein in medium trot. Working trot.	10
4.	A D	Turn onto the centre line. Leg yield right to between B and R.	10
5.	M MCH	Transition to working canter left. Working canter.	10
6.	HV VKA	Medium canter. Working canter.	10
7.	A AFP	Circle left 20 metres diameter. Give and retake the reins when crossing the centre line. Working canter.	10
8.	PXS SH H	Change the rein. Counter canter. Transition to working trot.	10
9.	HCMR R	Working trot. Circle right 15 metres diameter.	10
10.	RK K	Change the rein in medium trot. Working trot.	10
11.	A D	Turn onto the centre line. Leg yield left to between E and S.	10
12.	H HCM	Transition to working canter right. Working canter.	10
13.	MP PFA	Medium canter. Working canter.	10
14.	A AKV	Circle right 20 metres diameter. Give and retake the reins when crossing the centre line. Working canter.	10
15.	VXR RM M	Change the rein. Counter canter. Transition to working trot.	10
16.	C	Halt, immobility 3-5 seconds. Proceed in medium walk.	10
17.	HSXPF	Change the rein in free walk on a long rein.	10x2
18.	F A AKV	Medium walk. Transition to working trot. Working trot.	10

19.	VP P	Half circle right 20 metres diameter, allow the horse to seek the rein and stretch. Continue stretching.	10
20.	Before F A	Retake the reins. Turn onto the centre line.	10
21.	X	Halt, immobility, salute.	10
Leave the arena at walk on a long rein at a convenient place.			
22.		Paces	10
23.		Impulsion	10x2
24.		Submission	10x2
25.		Rider position and seat	10x2
			290

All trot work may be executed ‘sitting’ or ‘rising’.

Approximate time 5 1/2 minutes.

THE PONY CLUB INTRODUCTION TO DRESSAGE TEST 2019

20mx40m Arena

1.	A	Enter in working trot and proceed down the centre line without halting.	10
2.	C B	Turn right in working trot. Turn right, between X and E transition to medium walk.	10
3.	E K	Turn left in medium walk. Transition to working trot.	10
4.	B	Circle left 20m diameter and on second half of circle transition to working canter left.	10
5.	MCH	Working canter, between E and K transition to working trot.	10
6.	A	Medium walk.	10
7.	FX	Free walk on a long rein.	10x2
8.	Btwn X & H C	Medium walk. Working trot.	10
9.	B	Circle 20m diameter and on second half of circle transition to working canter right.	10
10.	FAK Btwn E & H	Working canter. Transition to working trot.	10
11.	MXK A	Change the rein in working trot. Down centre line.	10
12.	Btwn X & G	Halt and salute.	10
Leave arena at walk on a long rein at a suitable place.			
13.		Paces	10
14.		Impulsion	10x2
15.		Submission	10x2
16.		Rider position and seat	10x2
			200

All trot work may be executed 'sitting' or 'rising'.

Approximate time 4 1/2 minutes.

THE PONY CLUB GRASSROOTS PC80 TEST 2018

20mx40m Arena

1.	A	Enter in working trot and proceed down the centre line without halting.	10
2.	C	Track right.	10
3.	ME	Change the rein.	10
4.	A	Circle left 20m in working trot.	10
5.	FE	Change the rein.	10
6.	C	Circle right 20m in working trot.	10
7.	Btwn C & M	Medium walk.	10
8.	MXK	Free walk on a long rein. Just before K medium walk.	10
9.	Btwn K & A	Working trot.	10
10.	A	Circle left 20m and after crossing the centre line and before A working canter left.	10
11.	B	Circle left 20m and on the second half of the circle working trot.	10
12.	MCH	Working trot.	10
13.	HXF	Change the rein in working trot.	10
14.	A	Circle right 20m and after crossing the centre line and before A working canter right.	10
15.	E	Circle right 20m in working canter and on the second half of the circle working trot.	10
16.	HC	Working trot.	10
17.	M	Medium walk.	10
18.	B	Half circle 10m to X.	10
19.	G	Halt. Immobility. Salute.	10
Leave arena at walk on a long rein at a suitable place.			
20.		Paces	10
21.		Impulsion	10
22.		Submission	10
23.		Rider position and seat	10x2
			240

All trot work may be executed 'sitting' or 'rising'.

Approximate time 4 1/2 minutes.

THE PONY CLUB PRELIMINARY PC70 TEST 2022

20mx40m Arena

1.	A C	Enter at working trot and proceed down the centre line without halting. Turn right.	10
2.	MBF	Working trot.	10
3.	A	Circle right 20m diameter in working trot.	10
4.	KXM	Change the rein in working trot.	10
5.	C	Circle left 20m diameter in working trot.	10
6.	H HX	Medium walk. Medium walk.	10
7.	XF Btwn F & A	Free walk on a long rein. Medium walk.	10x2
8.	K	Working trot.	10
9.	E	Circle right 20m diameter and on the second half of the circle working canter right.	10
10.	EHCMB	Working canter.	10
11.	Btwn B & F	Working trot.	10
12.	KXM	Change the rein in working trot.	10
13.	E	Circle left 20m diameter and on the second half of the circle working canter left.	10
14.	EKAFB	Working canter.	10
15.	Btwn B & M	Working trot.	10
16.		Half circle 10m to X	10
17.	G	Halt and salute. The halt may be progressive through walk.	10
Leave the arena at free walk on a long rein at a convenient place.			
18.		Fluency of the transitions.	10
19.		Harmony between rider and pony.	10x2
20.		Rider's balance, straightness and suppleness.	10x2
21.		Rider's influence over the pony's way of going.	10x2
			250

All trot work to be executed 'sitting' or 'rising'.

Approximate time 5 minutes.

APPENDIX C – DIAGRAMS OF DRESSAGE ARENAS

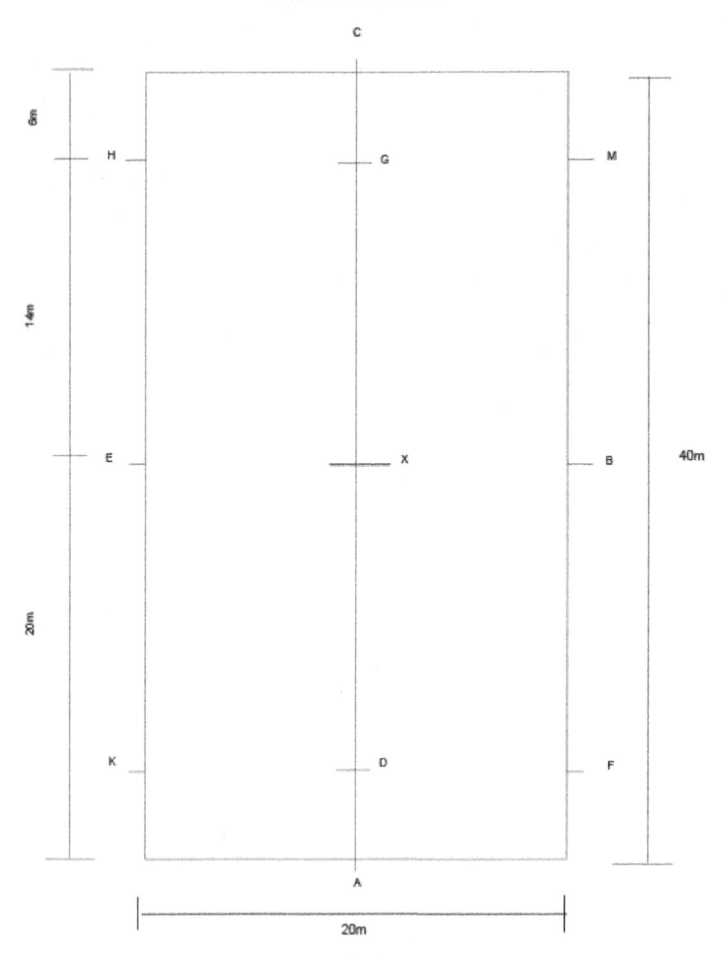

The length of the diagonal from corner to corner is 44.72m

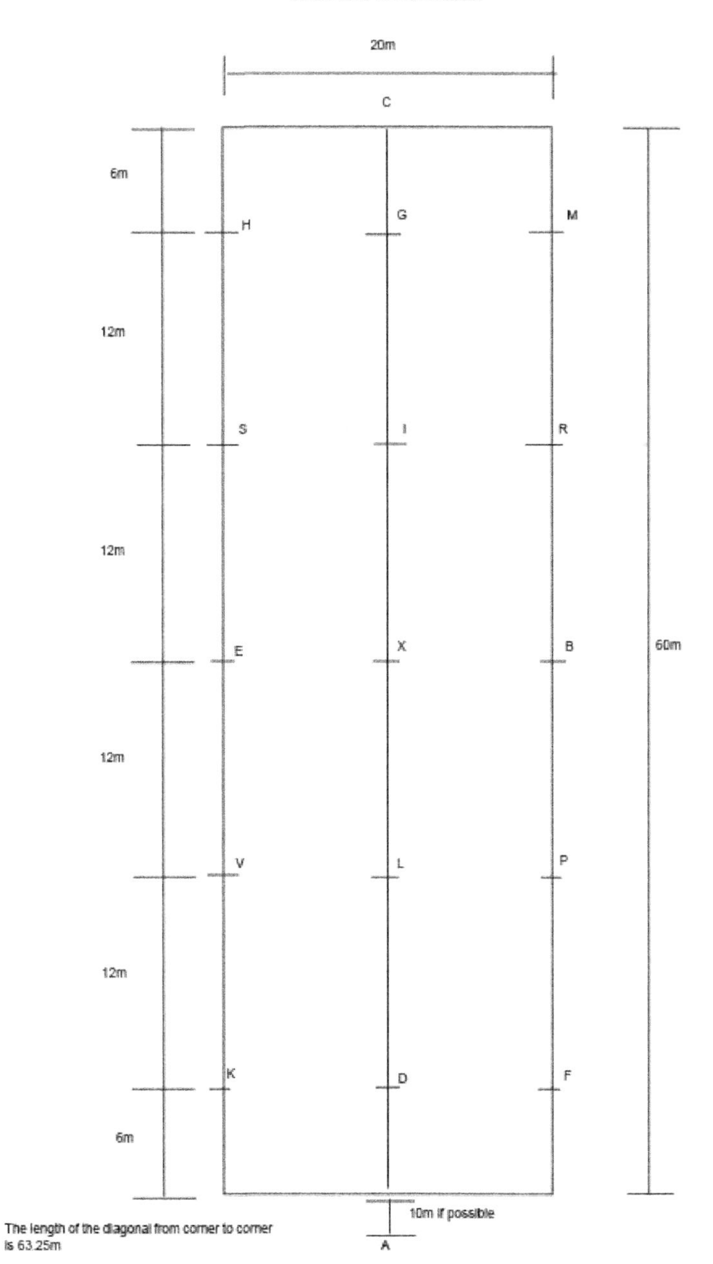
DIAGRAM OF 20 x 60m ARENA
20m
C
6m
H
G
M
12m
S
I
R
12m
E
X
B
60m
12m
V
L
P
12m
K
D
F
6m
10m if possible
A
The length of the diagonal from corner to corner is 63.25m

APPENDIX D – RULES FOR PONY CLUB TWO-DAY EVENTS

Introduction

The Dressage, Show Jumping and Cross Country Tests remain the same as in a Pony Club One-Day Horse Trial, and will be conducted in accordance with the Rules for Pony Club Eventing, but in this Competition, the Cross Country will become a PHASE of the SPEED AND ENDURANCE TEST.

The particular OBJECT of this type of competition will be to give riders experience in judging pace, preparing their horses before and caring for them during a Speed and Endurance Test. The speeds and distances set are well within the capabilities of the average pony.

Any such event will be valueless unless it is very well organised and strictly controlled (See Notes for Organisers). It is only suitable for the more experienced Members of The Pony Club (PC100 and PC110) who must be properly briefed before the start of the competition.

Rules

Except where modified below, a Pony Club Two-Day Event will be conducted in accordance with the Rules for Pony Club Eventing.

The Programme

Whenever possible the programme should be:

- 1st Day DRESSAGE followed by SHOW JUMPING TEST
- 2nd Day SPEED AND ENDURANCE

The Speed and Endurance Phase

This should consist of:

- PHASE A ROADS AND TRACKS
- PHASE B STEEPLECHASE
- PHASE C ROADS AND TRACKS
- PHASE D CROSS COUNTRY

Timing

Each phase must be timed independently. Separate starts and finishes are required for Phases A, B and D, and a separate finish for Phase C. The start of Phase C is the same as the finish of Phase B and competitors are not required to pause between these Phases. A competitor arriving late at the start of Phase B should be started as soon as possible at the discretion of the starter.

Independence of Phases

a) The different Phases A, B, C and D are quite independent of each other. Loss of time in one cannot be compensated for by gain of time in another.

b) The gain of one minute in Phase B (Steeplechase), for instance, does not give a competitor any more time in which to complete Phase C (Roads and Tracks), for which the starting time is identical with the finishing time of the Steeplechase. But if he then completes Phase C within the optimum time he obtains, due to the gain of one minute in the Steeplechase, one minute's rest and any time he has saved on Phase C, in addition to the 10 minutes compulsory halt provided for the second inspection before Phase D (Cross Country), the starting time for which is fixed by the timetable.

c) If a competitor completes Phase A in less than the optimum time and as a result arrives before the time fixed for starting Phase B (Steeplechase), he must wait until the time he gained has elapsed. The timekeeper starts him off on the Steeplechase at the exact time shown on the timetable.

d) If he finishes at exactly the right time, he immediately starts the Steeplechase.

e) If he has lost time during Phase A and if he finishes after the time fixed, according to the timetable, for the start of the Steeplechase, he must be started as soon as possible. The exact time at which he passes the starting post of Phase B is noted and the competitor is penalised for exceeding the optimum time for Phase A. He need not attempt to regain the time lost, since this is lost and penalised for Phase A and Phase A only.

f) The rest of this competitor's timetable will be affected by the time lost on Phase A but this will in no way affect the reckoning of the actual time he takes to complete the other phases.

g) If a competitor, having started the Steeplechase (Phase B) at the correct time, according to the timetable, exceeds the optimum time for this phase, it does not mean that he will have any less than the optimum time in which to complete Phase C or reduce the 10 minute compulsory halt, but the time at which he starts Phase D (Cross Country) can no longer correspond to the timetable laid down beforehand; it will differ by the amount of time lost on the Steeplechase.

h) It is possible that a competitor might exceed the optimum time for both Phase A and the Steeplechase. In this case, his time of starting Phase D will be delayed for as long as the two excesses of time added together for which he has been penalised.

10 Minute Halt

This will be between the end of Phase C and the start of Phase D and is compulsory. A competitor who arrives early at the end of Phase C will have a correspondingly longer halt.

A steward will inspect all horses at the end of Phase C. If he is in any doubt as to whether a horse is fit to continue the horse must be examined by a Vet.

Roads and Tracks

a) TOTAL distance for the two phases will be between 4,800m and 8,400m.

b) OPTIMUM TIME for Phase A will be achieved at a speed of 220m. per min. Phase C will be achieved at a speed of 160m. per min.

EXCEEDING the Optimum Time incurs 1 penalty for each second up to a TIME LIMIT which is 1/5 more than the optimum time.

c) DIRECTION MARKERS AND BOUNDARY MARKERS shall be used. Km. Markers will be put out to assist competitors.

d) Competitors may dismount anywhere and walk or run beside the horse, but must be mounted to pass through the finish.

Steeplechase

a) DISTANCE will be 1,000m

b) THE COURSE will consist of 5 or 6 obstacles with wings.

c) OPTIMUM TIME will be achieved at a speed of 500m per min. Exceeding the Optimum Time incurs 1 penalty for each commenced period of 3 seconds up to a TIME LIMIT of twice the OPTIMUM TIME.

d) Boundary/Direction Markers will be the same as for the Cross Country and all obstacles will be numbered.

e) Faults incurred at obstacles will be the same as for Cross Country obstacles.

f) Type of obstacles – Bush or Gorse covered fences of the type used in Point-to-Point Steeplechases should be used. They must look imposing and be very well sloped.

g) Dimensions of obstacles will be the same as for the Cross Country obstacles EXCEPT that the solid part of a steeplechase fence between the boundary flags must not exceed 60cm in height, and the width shall be at least 3.75m.

Cross Country

The Course should conform to The Pony Club Eventing Rules.

Qualifications

a) HORSES/PONIES - There is no height limit.

All horses must have been regularly ridden at rallies by a member of the Pony Club.

Horses that are graded British Eventing Advanced (Grade 1) that have completed at AI/A level during the current calendar year are not eligible. No horse under 5 years of age is eligible.

b) District Commissioners are required to certify personally for each individual event that all riders entered are eligible

APPENDIX E – HEAD INJURY AND CONCUSSION FLOWCHART

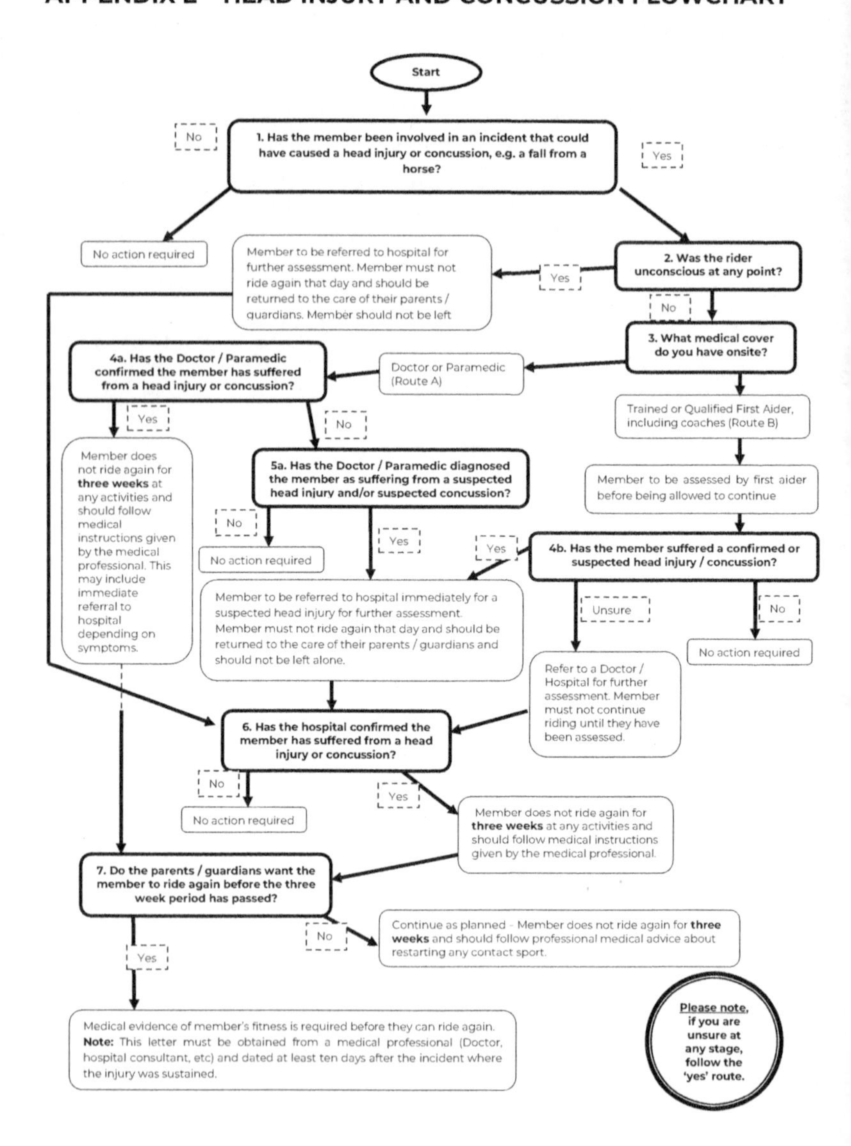

Start
1. Has the member been involved in an incident that could have caused a head injury or concussion, e.g. a fall from a horse?
No
Yes
No action required
2. Was the rider unconscious at any point?
Yes
Member to be referred to hospital for further assessment. Member must not ride again that day and should be returned to the care of their parents / guardians. Member should not be left
No
3. What medical cover do you have onsite?
Doctor or Paramedic (Route A)
Trained or Qualified First Aider, including coaches (Route B)
4a. Has the Doctor / Paramedic confirmed the member has suffered from a head injury or concussion?
Yes
No
Member does not ride again for **three weeks** at any activities and should follow medical instructions given by the medical professional. This may include immediate referral to hospital depending on symptoms.
5a. Has the Doctor / Paramedic diagnosed the member as suffering from a suspected head injury and/or suspected concussion?
No
No action required
Yes
Member to be assessed by first aider before being allowed to continue
Yes
4b. Has the member suffered a confirmed or suspected head injury / concussion?
Member to be referred to hospital immediately for a suspected head injury for further assessment. Member must not ride again that day and should be returned to the care of their parents / guardians and should not be left alone.
Unsure
No
No action required
Refer to a Doctor / Hospital for further assessment. Member must not continue riding until they have been assessed.
6. Has the hospital confirmed the member has suffered from a head injury or concussion?
No
No action required
Yes
Member does not ride again for **three weeks** at any activities and should follow medical instructions given by the medical professional.
7. Do the parents / guardians want the member to ride again before the three week period has passed?
No
Continue as planned - Member does not ride again for **three weeks** and should follow professional medical advice about restarting any contact sport.
Yes
Medical evidence of member's fitness is required before they can ride again.
Note: This letter must be obtained from a medical professional (Doctor, hospital consultant, etc) and dated at least ten days after the incident where the injury was sustained.
Please note, if you are unsure at any stage, follow the 'yes' route.

Chav Christianity

By

Darren Edwards

Published by New Generation Publishing in 2013

First Edition

Bible passages used are from the NIV bible.

www.newgeneration-publishing.com

New Generation **Publishing**

Table of Contents

Foreword

In 1996 I started a brand new church from scratch on a council estate in Essex. Being a Romford boy by birth and having spent all of my life until that point in time in Essex I thought I would know a thing or two about sharing my relatively new faith with people from God's own county.

At the time, church planting, although taking place up and down the country was not as fashionable as it is now and there wasn't a huge amount of material written about it. Much of what was available was pretty middle class in outlook and narrative but I guess that was to be expected as most of the churches in the UK were pretty much middle class anyway. I remember being given one book that was about 150 pages long which was billed as "the complete guide to church planting." I didn't realise then just how ridiculous that title was. Nothing was to prepare me, as a guy in his early 20s for what my wife and I were to encounter.

After several years, a new church was up and running and I was a different man. I had seen brokenness and despair in people that I hadn't been prepared for. From severe alcohol abuse, to the effects of long term unemployment to domestic violence, drugs and a lack of educational opportunity and understanding we had encountered a community that had a kind of hopelessness over it. The gospel radically changed that and as we saw the message of Jesus impact peoples lives, so we saw the local community start to change.

Despite this apparent success I was, however, left with a vague feeling that something wasn't right. We had failed in a very significant area. We hadn't raised up local leaders. This is perhaps one of my biggest regrets of those years. We had tried but we hadn't succeeded at all.

That is why this book by Darren Edwards is so important. Not only do you see the story of a man redeemed but you are also witnessing within these pages, a man raised up by God to lead and establish churches amongst his own. The denomination of the so called "chav" is well documented. Darren is one of the answers. The UK church has failed to reach into the white working class to an epic degree. What you see here is part of the solution in front of our very eyes.

The book is raw, honest and reads as if Darren is sitting next to you in the cafe over a mug of tea. If you want an insight and a window into chav culture and a glimpse of hope of what could be, then I urge you to read this timely book. Lets cheer this guy on and pray that in the years to come we read a sequel that speaks of not one church but many churches across the UK pioneering as Darren is.

Carl Beech
Christian Vision for Men.
@carlfbeech

Introduction

Before I get carried away with writing this book, let me first explain why I chose to write it and why I chose the title – '*Chav Christianity: Exploring what it looks like to be a working-class Christian*'. Sat in my front room at Regents Theological College, listening to a classic song – '*Many Rivers To Cross*' by UB40 – I can't help but look around me and notice that '*I'm the only chav in the village*'[1]. Needless to say that there are a lot of Christians like myself that come from a working-class background and most are encouraged to conform to the likeness of their friends at church, and change the way they behave to suit middle-class etiquette.[2] In most cases we are trained to think, act, and dress like our middle-class Christian counterparts. However, in my walk I have made a conscious effort to keep my heritage and way of life – I have downright refused to give up my culture and

---

1 Although not technically, as during our first year of bible college a young man moved into the village surrounding the college. My wife and I laughed as anxiety struck the college and some brave students decided to protect the college campus by acting as security guards in the evenings to deter the young lad from trying to steal cars. No offence if you were one of those students or the chav in question.

2 Derek Purnell, Phone conversation with author, 19th December 2012.

upbringing, I refuse to be changed into a politically correct lesser image of myself, and in doing so I have come to realise that it is possible to be a Christian chav.

Right now I'd like to point out that this book is not trying to claim that being a working-class Christian is any better than being a middle-class Christian. It is simply pointing out some ways in which we can learn to grow into a well-rounded Christian chav, and hopefully helping other urban missionaries to understand the people that they are working with.

This book is being written on the back of a dissertation devoted to the working-class mission, and spirituality. Whilst writing the paper I was able to find many sources of information that strengthened my conviction that there is a clear divide between the classes, and in many cases there are prejudices between the classes,[3] even amongst Christians. Although we don't like to admit it, and we shouldn't glorify it, we should be aware of the issue and try to use our knowledge of it accordingly. This book will highlight some of those differences and

3 All you have to do is listen to popular rapper Plan B's album, *Ill Manors*, or read some popular books written by some critics of the chav culture to see this; L. Bok, *The Little Book of Chavs*, (Crombie: Jardine Publishing Limited, 2004); M. Wallace & C. Spanner, *Chav: A user's guide to Britain's new ruling class*, (London: Bantam Books, 2004).

prejudices in the hope that we as Christians can direct our mission, teaching, and lifestyles to expand the Church's influence in society as a whole. Ultimately if you are working-class, this book is here to tell you that it is ok to remain working-class, and that you have a purpose as a working-class Christian. You could be the difference between life and death for approximately 50% of our nation. According to the BBC, a British Social Attitudes survey found that 57% of adults in Britain believe themselves to be working-class,[4] despite middle-class politicians and journalists flooding the airwaves with words like *"we're all middle-class now"* (John Prescott), or *"the class war is over, and we won it!"* (David Cameron).[5]

In 1973 John Bennington, a community worker from Coventry, wrote a book on class and Christian beliefs. In the book he claims that if we were to take a snapshot of the British church, we might wonder if John Calvin was right about election and whether God is attracted to the middle-classes. This is because as we look around the church we see that it is highly populated by those from

4 BBC News Magazine, 'What is working class?', http://news.bbc.co.uk/1/hi/magazine/6295743.stm, accessed 14th May 2013.

5 O. Jones, *Chavs: The demonization of the working class,* (London: Verso, 2011), 44.

the middle-class. Using various statistics, he claims that it is not that the working-class are irreligious, but implies that they simply do not fit into the normal church model – apparently 71% of working-class people who took a survey said that salvation comes through Jesus, compared to 59% of middle-class people who were asked the same question. He claims that only 2.5% of working-class converts manage to keep their faith and their culture, and the rest tend to fall away or receive a '*class transplant.*' Basically, of the 97% of working-class people that join the church, the majority become pretty much indistinguishable from the class that they mix with – they become middle-class to fit in with the norms of church life.[6] Fundamentally, in the same way in which we believe the best way to do mission in foreign countries is to learn their language and culture to better present a relevant gospel, we need to be able to talk, dress, and act working-class in order to present a relevant gospel to over half of our nation. This can be achieved more effectively by someone who already understands what it means to be working-class, and how to think like a working-class person. Someone that is committed to being a chav for chavs, or a Jew to the Jews (1 Corinthians 9:20).

---

6 J. Bennington, *Culture, Class & Christian Beliefs*, (London: Scripture Union, 1973), 15-16.

Barbara Ellen, writing for The Observer, gives a compelling argument against this fascination that middle-England has with people moving away from their working-class roots. In an article – named *You stay working class all your life, so be proud of it* – she attacks the assumption that being working-class is something to be ashamed of – like the government and journalism across our nation world have you believe. As she comes to an end she tells her readers:

> *"It's as if the successful working classes have been silenced, bullied and mocked into dismissing their own origins as irrelevant. Indeed, why is Melvyn Bragg left groping for bizarre self-definitions ("class-mongrel") – why can't he simply be defined as a high-achieving, literate, working-class man?'*[7]

We shouldn't be mocked, or scared, into changing our way of life in order to follow Jesus. We are transformed by the Holy Spirit, and cultivated through the discipleship of our community (Proverbs 27:17). From the moment you began your spiritual journey the Holy Spirit has been transforming you, now it is time for you to cultivate your spirituality – your chav spirituality! I

---

7 Barbara Ellen, The Observer, '*You stay working class all your life, so be proud of it,*' http://www.guardian.co.uk/commentisfree/2012/feb/26/barbara-ellen-your-class-stays-with-you, accessed 24th May 2013.

guess what I'm saying is that I want to encourage you to be you, and to get to know yourself better. What makes you tick, why you do the things you do, and why it will attract others that do the same. To finish I will quote Roy Joslin – writer of *Urban Harvest*:

> *"Until some more effective way of appealing to the artisan has been found there will be no real revival of religion in this country."*[8]

---

8 R. Joslin, *Urban Harvest: Biblical perspectives on Christian mission in the inner cities*, (Welwyn: Evangelical Press, 1982), 1.

Chav: The Definition

We've all heard the term '*chav*' used in our culture. It seems that everyone is able to point out a chav, but no-one claims to be one. In fact, as far as many people are concerned, there is not a definite meaning for the word. I will try to give an idea of what the term means to certain groups of people, and then I'll try to explain how I intend to use it in this book.

Middle-class journalists and professionals have been known to use the term 'chav' in a derogatory manner towards the working-class population in the UK. Owen Jones wrote an award winning book in 2011 titled *Chavs: The demonization of the working-class,* in which he explains at length the way in which the government, and journalists, have been using the lower-classes as scapegoats since the days of Thatcher.[9] His book will be used at length, along with other secular books and research throughout this book.

---

9 Jones, *Chavs*.

Cambridge Dictionaries Online lists a chav as '*an insulting word for someone, usually a young person, whose way of dressing, speaking, and behaving is thought to show their lack of education and low social class*'.[10]

For this reason it is easy to see why no-one would want to call themselves a chav. Indeed, a really close friend of mine – who most would claim is a stereotypical chav – recently 'blasted' a local lad, for an act of anti-social behaviour, by calling him "*stupid little chav*", finishing his rant by telling me how much he hates 'them', and is glad that he isn't one.

Throughout this book the word chav will be used to describe those that fall into the lower-classes, but will not be used in a derogatory manner. At this point I would like to make clear that I, Darren Edwards, am a chav and that I am extremely proud to be one. I love my culture, I love my life, I love my family, and I love my estate. The aim of this book is to let every other chav, or lower-class, person know that it is still alright to be proud of your values, etiquette, and culture – after all there are some values amongst the lower-classes that better represent Jesus' values than some of those of the middle-classes.

---

10 Cambridge Dictionaries Online, '*Chav*', http://dictionary.cambridge.org/dictionary/british/chav, accessed 16th May 2013.

You do not have to fit in with the world in order to be accepted by it, and you don't have to fit into the church in order to be accepted by it. I want you to be the chaviest, most explosive, loyal, flamboyant, funny, and unorthodox Christian to ever grace our beautiful country.

Chris Haylett, a lecturer a Birmingham University, wrote:

> *"My politics are not derived from workplace, region or formal education. They are the politics of my home, of growing up through the 1980s on council estates in the south of England, talking back at the telly, sitting in waiting rooms of the Department of Social Security, and watching mum go in and out of hospital. My class positionality is not only about a lack of money (although economically things aren't good enough), and it does not seek 'inclusion' to things middle class. In some respects my politics are private: a politics of finding pleasure in certain kinds of music and films as cultural affirmation of who I am, or imagine myself to be in relation to others. In other respects they are quite traditional: a politics of pride and anger, of*

> *personal and collective memory, a defence against division and against attack."*[11]

It's time to start our journey to explore what a proudly working-class Christian looks like, and how we can be more like Jesus, instead of having to conform to middle-England's expectations and aspirations.

---

11 Chris Haylett, "'This is about us, this is our film!': Personal and popular discourses of 'Underclass'," *in Cultural Studies And The Working Class*, ed. Sally R. Munt, (London: Cassell, 2000), 69-70.

My Story

My story starts on a council estate in Northampton, a large town in the midlands with over 200,000 residents. My mum tells me that the day she told my dad that she was pregnant with me, he went to get some cigarettes from the shop and never came back – I think that this was her way of telling me that he wasn't interested in being a father, especially as they were both quite young. My childhood, as you could guess, was a fatherless one and before long my young mother couldn't cope with looking after me, along with my siblings – who would come soon after. Social services reports claim that one of the neighbours had caught me stealing bread from their bird table for me and my siblings to eat, and they subsequently put a lot of effort into keeping us safe.

My Nan's House

Aged seven, after a previous attempt at getting custody of me, my nan managed to get the courts and my mum to agree to give her full custody of me. Before long I was living with my grandparents and my uncle Johnathan. It was whilst living with my nan that things changed in my life – unlike my mum who didn't have much time to show me love, my nan would quite literally shower me with love, often hugging and kissing me, although this would often get embarrassing in front of my friends.

My pap, John, was the father figure I had been missing and he introduced me to loving discipline. As I think about him I get a lump in my throat. One of my oldest memories is of my pap telling me things like "*real men don't hit women*" and "*anyone can make a little girl, but it takes a real man to raise one.*" These along with many other of life's lessons that he taught me have stuck with me throughout my life, and went on to make a huge difference in who I am today. Coincidently, it was this idea that it takes a real man to raise a little girl that caused me to send my children to church with my wife, Laura, later on in life. I wanted my children to have the very best opportunity that they could, even though in some cases it meant that they would be different from me.

Needless to say, I still wasn't exactly a well rounded young man and I would often get angry, lashing out at anyone that crossed my path. This became a way of life for me and at times I would think that my options in life were '*hurt or be hurt... bully or be bullied,*' meaning I would often get into fights – getting suspended from school, and losing friends as quickly as I made them in a lot of cases.

Becoming A Young Adult

Being a bit of a brawler, and known for being loud, I soon fitted into the stereotypical cast of a chav. It wasn't long before I was drinking and taking some drugs, after all drinking, smoking, and drugs were not frowned upon by my mum rather they were almost glorified. The more my grandparents tried to discipline me, the more I tugged the other way. What's more, my mum was back in Northampton telling me that I was able to move back in with her as soon as I turned fifteen. I became more rebellious and pushed the boundaries more and more everyday.

Aged fifteen, my grandparents decided it would be good to invite my sister round on a night that I was meant to be sleeping at a friends house. They didn't know it but we were actually going to camp in the playing field smoking hash and drinking. So when they announced the new plan – for my sister to stay round so that we could spend some time together – I made the decision to stay out with my friends for the night. When I went home the next day my sister, probably hearing it from my mum, told my nan that I had decided to move out and go back to

Northampton. On the back of my grandma's questions and emotions, and my own arrogant pride, I told my grandparents that I was moving back in with my mum. That day I packed a small bag full of clothes, purchased Eminem's album *The Marshall Mathers LP*, and spent the rest of my savings on a taxi to Northampton.

The day that I moved out, I remember it vividly, my pap sat on the edge of his bed with his head in his hands and just whispered to my nan *"I always knew it was going to happen!"* He had poured so much into my life, and had loved me like a son. It should be said that John wasn't my nan's first husband, and wasn't my biological grandfather, which makes his love and kindness even more amazing. It was about a year after I had moved back to Northampton that my pap died of cancer, and one of the last things he had said to me during that period was *"I'm still proud of you"* as he, almost ceremonially, presented me with his favourite Max Factor aftershave – every time my children smell it on me they ask me where we're going, knowing that it will be somewhere special. There are things in life that we will always be ashamed of, and hurting my pap with my pride and arrogance will be one of those for me.

Moving Back Home

One of the most important factors to moving back home was that there was no longer anyone that I respected, I had no boundaries, and there was a whole new world of drugs and crime for me to get involved in. Before long I was selling marijuana and stealing cars. My friends more or less had the same aspirations as me – which were basically to have as much fun as possible, without worrying about who we hurt, and to be as bad as possible. The consensus among the lads was that the rougher someone was, the more they should be respected. Once again this meant brawling and pushing the boundaries to see how much we could hurt someone, or how much we could steal. We would often spend a whole night stealing cars and racing them around.

One night we decided that we were going to have a party, but because we couldn't afford food we stole a car and drove up to a house that was used by a local Christian organisation. The house was on a farm, and was never locked up at night because there were a lot of Christians living there that would work lots of different shifts. We filled our boot with boxes of sandwiches and cakes, and started making our way home. On this occasion one of our tyres got punctured and we got arrested whilst fixing it and stealing another car.

It was about the same point in my life that my girlfriend, now my wife Laura, fell pregnant with my son. My mum was evicted from our home due to my anti-social behaviour, and so we ended up moving around a few different homes until Laura and I moved into Spencer – the housing estate that I started on as boy. This was a great joy to me because all of my family and lots of friends lived on the estate. Life calmed down slightly and I stopped stealing cars, but if you asked my friends today what I was like before becoming a Christian they would tell you that I was a brawler, drinker, and general lads lad that was willing to do anything for a laugh. Riding mini-motors and driving round like a nutter, even when I had been drinking heavily, was a normal occurrence. Although I still dabbled in drugs, my main issue was violence and alcoholism. On one occasion my friend had asked me to be his best man, in typical '*Darren style*' I drank myself into oblivion – spending £160 after abusing the free bar for half a day – before trying to drive my van home. On the way out of the venue I turned right, instead of left, and found myself sitting in a muddy field in my work-van patting myself down to make sure I had not hurt myself. I made it home that night only by what I would now call the grace of God.

My Spiritual Journey

We moved into our house on Spencer estate when Laura had just given birth to our daughter, Sophie. I had managed a clothing store in the town centre, aptly named Reefer, and soon got a job managing a flooring shop. We spent the next few years living a normal working-class life, our children went to the local school that I had attended as a child, and I moved on to managing another flooring shop before building my own business – selling and fitting flooring. It was during this time that Laura had begun attending church. I insisted that she took the children to Sunday School whilst my friends and I went to the fields, riding motorbikes.

Before long, Liam and Sophie were behaving like God was real, and Sophie had recently prayed that God would change the weather. Weirdly enough, God seemed to answer Sophie's prayers and, on three occasions, had changed the weather. About the same time, I happened to watch a program on the TV about the ark of the covenant. A presenter was trying to find a long-lost religious article and had taken DNA tests, and searched archaeological research, to find it. I found this fascinating as I was already wondering whether it was God who had answered Sophie's prayers, or if it was just a coincidence – although I thought that three coincidences with the same person was a little suspect. The presenter's search had led him to a small museum in Africa, and a drum that he claimed was the ark of the covenant. Fascinated by his findings I had to read the bible to see if he was right – what's more, was the bible right?

My problem was that I had heard the bible was translated and changed over the past two to six thousand years. There was no way that I was going to read a modern bible, so I prayed my first prayer – '*God if you're there, give me the book you want me to read and I'll read it.*' Within a couple of days, without me telling anyone about my prayer, my mother-in-law came to our house bringing with her an old lectern bible. This book was over 140 years old, and was so big that I would get cramps in my neck from reading it. The coincidental thing about this story is that Laura didn't even know that I was interested in God, she was out when I watched the program on TV, and had absolutely no idea about my fascination. It came as a total shock to everyone when I actually started reading the bible. Before long I had made a pact with Laura – if she let me play golf with my close friend John on Saturdays, I would go to church with her on Sunday mornings. I think she thought that this was an opportunity that she couldn't miss, whilst I was thinking that I was winning on both fronts.

At church I would sit in the balcony and would disappear as soon as the service was over – some time before that I walked out of the nativity play once my kids had done their bit so that I could watch United play Watford, much to Laura's horror. Whilst sitting through the church services there was two things that would happen to me. The first being that the preacher seemed to answer all my questions about God and religion as, or soon after, I had begun to ask them. The second thing that happened was that during the songs, I would become emotional. One of the songs had the lyrics:

> *"Every blessing you pour out I'll turn back to praise*
> *When the darkness closes in, Lord*
> *Still I will say, blessed be your name."*

As the people around me sang this song, I would find myself thinking: '*I have a beautiful wife, beautiful kids, a great family who I love, and I love where I live – wow! I've been blessed.*" It makes sense that I felt like it would be an injustice not to bless God by singing this song to him and many others that were being sung in the church. I found myself crying in secret on more than one occasion, and soon became convinced by all of the coincidences that were happening around my children, church, and friends as I began to pray for miracles.

In October 2008, after beginning to read the bible, I began to feel the same way about God that I did about my pap. God didn't come across to me as a strict, all powerful being, who hated me. Instead he came across as a father who, wanting the best for his children, had to discipline them in certain areas of life in the same way that I would tell my own children not to play with fire so that they would not get hurt. I began asking God why he was only showing himself to me now, and where he had been for the rest of my life. I remember falling asleep on my sofa reading the bible and God became real in my dreams as I began to see him with me, keeping me strong, and forming me throughout my entire life. It was at this point that I realised that I was never fatherless – God was my father and he had loved me and protected me on so many occasions. Two weeks later, I was invited to a men's night where we would watch England play Macedonia and have pie and chips with the blokes at church. I knew God was real, and had come to love him intensely, but did not know about Jesus. I only knew what people had told me in the past, I had not read that far in my bible, but knew that at some point I would read about him and would decide then whether he fitted the prophecies in the Old Testament. After the football a man by the name of George Miller, a well known evangelist in Elim, got up to preach a message of salvation, whilst he was doing so

God began to speak to me and I had a massive urge to become a Christian that night – I had researched what it meant to be a Christian, and had come to the conclusion that if I asked Jesus to forgive me for the things I had done wrong in my life and ask him to give me a new start, make me born again, he would answer and God would make me a new person with a fresh start. I had also read a lot in the bible and on the internet about how to live a lifestyle of holiness. I knew that it was those things that I had done wrong in my life that Jesus had been punished for, and so if Jesus was really who the bible says he was, he was also my father in a weird sort of way because the bible says that he was God in the flesh. All I knew is that I never wanted to hurt my father, God, like I did my pap and so I needed as much help as I could get. From what I understood, the bible told me that once I was born again God's Spirit could live within me so that I could say no to all the temptations that were thrown at me.

That night, after the football, I asked God to make me born again – to give me a clean slate and make me a new creation – and fill me with his Holy Spirit to keep me from ever hurting him again. That night he showed just how real he was, I cried out loud in front of people for the first time in years, and God's Holy Spirit 'knocked me for six'. It felt like there was electricity running through every part of my body, and I was shaking all over. It felt like DTs (delirium tremens, that alcoholics often experience when they stop drinking), which is another weird coincidence because that night I stopped drinking alcohol. I went from drinking a minimum of four cans of beer per day – and sometimes a whole crate – to nothing overnight, with what seemed to be no withdrawal symptoms. Laura wasn't there that night but, when I went home afterwards with her brother, she just knew that something had happened. Laura, her mum, and her aunty were sitting in the lounge and just took one look at me before asking '*what's happened to you?*' I was just trying to act as normal as possible. A couple of weeks down the line, Laura had noticed a massive change and had realised how real God was. My attitude had totally changed, and all I could think about was God. I was running my own business and so just put work to one side, going to church everyday seeking discipleship from my pastor. It wasn't long before they locked me out of the church and told me to get a job.

After Being Born Again

Needless to say, my life changed and I became totally obsessed with God and the bible. I got involved with lots of ministries and began to serve God in many different respects. In July 2010 I moved to Malvern, in Worcestershire, where I would start a 3 year degree in applied theology. It wasn't long after starting that I realised I was a little different from other Christians in churches, and at bible college. I refused to conform to the normal way of being a Christian, and wanted to explore for myself what being a Christian looked like for me. It's not that there is anything wrong with normal Christians, or churches for that matter. It was just that I saw Jesus through different eyes and understood sin slightly differently. For example, many Christians seem to have a twisted view of pride, but when I read the bible I saw that it often says that it is ok to take pride in what you do. It just so happens that I am proud of quite a lot of things – I'm proud of my background, I'm proud of my gifts, I'm proud of my strengths, and I'm proud of my family. It just seems a little backwards that God would tell me not to be proud of something that he has given me.

When I spent three years studying theology, church history, and how to apply it all to my ministry and life, one of the things I was taught is the idea of organic church. This is the notion that for churches to better reach non-believers from different cultures they may need to grow out of the culture that is already present in a place, or community. When someone in that community becomes a believer, church should grow out of their understanding of worship, teaching, and discipleship. Thinking with this mindset, I came up with the idea of chav church. I, myself, would be the beginnings of an organic church. A chav off the estate exploring what a chav church would look like constitutes the exact representation of organic church as I understood it, and so in the summer of 2013 my family and I began pioneering a chav church in Lincoln. I would love to tell you about lots of miracles and successful ministry opportunities that my colleagues and I have had since that time, but I would also like to make this book as accessible as possible too. At the end of this book I will make a point of recommending some further reading to help you to understand yourself, other people, and God's plan or vision for your life too.

Part of being a chav church includes exploring what it looks like to be a working-class, or chav, Christian. This brings us up to date with where this book is at right now. The next few chapters will look to discover the main characteristics of working-class people, and offer ways in which we can cultivate those differences in culture to best advance the gospel. I would also like to help people that are not part of working-class culture to understand why we do the things we do so that they can disciple us better, and work alongside us more effectively.

It would be crazy for me to let this moment pass without giving you the opportunity to start your very own spiritual journey – maybe a chav one. If you've been feeling like there must be more to life than what you currently see and my story, along with some others, has made you inquisitive to find out more about God, or maybe you are more sure than that and want to make a decision to go after God seeking him and trying to live for him. You can start your journey now by saying a quick prayer and then telling someone what you have done. The prayer is simple, you just have to say something like '***God I want to follow you and get to know you. I'm sorry for the things that I've done that have hurt you or others, and I want you to help me to be the best me that I can be. Give me all the help from heaven that I need! Amen.***'

If you are able to tell someone that you've begun a spiritual journey and a relationship with God, then find a nearby church where you can explore some more, that would be awesome.

Fundamental Values & Beliefs

Each class brings with it hidden rules, and values. Even though an individual may become more affluent many of their patterns of thought, social interaction, and cognitive strategies will remain the same.[12] These hidden rules are the unspoken habitual behaviours and values that cause us to act in particular ways.[13] For example, the way that the classes receive and appreciate food can be quite different for what some of us may consider simple reasons – a working-class individual may well look at the food asking '*was there enough*', whereas a middle-class person would ask '*did you like it?*' or '*is it good for you?*' and those from the higher classes would ask '*how was it presented?*'[14] Right now you may be recognising these assertions amongst your family and friends, and be putting yourself into a social class. Additionally, you may take a few minutes to wonder why this is so – why do you think, and act, that way? This chapter will look at some

---

12 R. K. Payne, *A Framework For Understanding Poverty*, (Highlands: Aha! Process Inc., 1996), 11.

13 *Ibid*, 52

14 *Ibid*, 59

of the fundamental differences that could be cultivated to enhance our spiritual walk, and bring us closer to God. You may not be able to tick every box in this book. That is good because God made all of us individuals, and this book aims to celebrate those differences. Some of the more prominent areas of difference will be looked at more closely in the chapters after this one in order to get a better look at them.

Aspirations

In my first year of bible college, during a lecture on management and leadership, my lecturer explained to the class that whilst growing up as a young pentecostal pastor's son he lived on the rough streets of Manchester. As he grew up and pentecostals became more mainstream and affluent, the people around them at church encouraged them to move into a nicer area. The reasons were the same as we hear from churches today, and anyone from the middle-classes – your children will get better opportunities in more affluent areas, and '*why would you want to stay in that area anyway?*' The majority of people, no matter what culture they grow up in, will undoubtedly be conformed into the image of the dominant group in their locality.[15] For many people in

---

15 T. Chester, *Unreached: Growing churches in working-class and deprived areas*, (Nottingham: Inter-Varsity Press, 2012), 34.

the UK this means being told that the only credible aspirations available to us is to become upper-middle class. For this reason we are told that education is important, everyone should own their home, and anyone can work their way out of poverty.[16] For our traditional lower-classes however, aspirations differ.

UB40, named after the *Unemployment Benefit, Form 40* that was once used to 'sign-on',[17] are a great example of working-class aspirations. The band, even after breaking through in the world of music and selling thousands of records, kept their working-class roots and values. Ali and Robin Campbell put their views down to their granddad's appetite for justice, telling the readers in their autobiography:

> *"Grandad was a very proud man, staunch socialist, passionate trade unionist and all-round champion of the working man."*[18]

Ali and Robin's dad was also a very well known music artist, who, despite all of his fame still lived in a council house and brought the lads up there.[19] The two of them

---

16 Jones, *Chavs*, 6-12.

17 UB40: The Official Site, '*The History: Introduction,*' http://www.ub40.co.uk/introduction.html, accessed 19th May 2013.

18 R. Campbell & A. Campbell, *Blood and Fire*, (London: Arrow Books LTD, 2006), 3.

19 *Ibid*, 11.

tell of how the children at school would not believe them when they said who their dad was because they still lived in a council house, and so they would get tired of trying to explain – telling their friends that their dad was a dustbin man.

An American sociologist, Ruby Payne, explains that for the working-class, aspirations are different. Instead of aspiring to have a large house, or a good career, the majority of people from the lower-classes aspire to have large families or a large network of friends.[20] Working-class aspirations tend to be more relational than material. When I asked a hundred working-class people about their aspirations, they confirmed this to be the case – showing that material wealth is not as important to those from the lower-classes. Payne highlights that for the lower-classes, people are the most important possession available. Things may be this way because on many estates around our country money is hard to come by, which means that we have to rely on each other for help in times of need. Material possessions are quickly handed over to one another, without a second thought, because at a later date we may need the same sort of grace. For a working-class Christian this would mean improving the quality of friends and relationships in your life, in

---

20 Payne, *Understanding Poverty*, 59.

comparison to someone who is middle-class that may believe improving their life means improving the quality of the material things that surround them – this could require improving their house, or moving to a pleasant area.

With this in mind, I will explore how we can best utilise our aspirations for God's calling on our lives, and how we can use them for the benefit of the Kingdom of God. One thing that we must keep in mind is our family and friends. As a working-class Christian you are going to be feeling more emotionally attached to your family and friends than what you may have done before. You have previously lived with the saying '*blood is thicker than water*,'[21] and this is true for the majority of people living on housing estates. However, now you have God's emotions running through your body, and you love your community in a deeper way. There will be people around you at church that will encourage you to move up the social ladder and move out of your community, but I want to tell you to stay. The bible says that we should remain in the situation that we were in when God saved us (1 Corinthians 7:20-21). The best person to introduce

21 Meaning that family bonds are stronger than any bonds with outsiders; The Phrase Finder, '*Blood is thicker than water*,' http://www.phrases.org.uk/meanings/67600.html, accessed 20th May 2013.

your family and friends to Jesus is you. As time goes by you'll find that the emotions you feel for your family become more and more real and, if you move now, you may find yourself regretting doing so in the future because you will know that no 'outsider' will be accepted as well as you will be, even though you may take some stick for your faith. If salvation is going to come to working-class Britain, it will come through those that know the culture, and have already been accepted into the community. Our estates don't need do-gooders, they need working-class Christians with a relevant and real spirituality. Just like UB40 won the hearts of the nation by painting their colours to the mast, you will do the same for your community.

A colleague at my bible college wrote a short note about his experience of becoming a Christian and leaving his friends behind. Mike Edwards wrote:

> *"It continually saddens me to see the Church, particularly evangelical, attempting to pull people out of their particular sub-culture. We seem to think we have a responsibility to make everyone middle-class, white and exceptionally well behaved. However this does not constitute mission for me. By pulling 'lower class' people out of pubs, or equally taking bankers away*

from their greedy friends, we miss the notion of incarnation. We need to understand the exceptional relevance of their testimony in their contexts, and work with that."

He continues:

"Upon becoming a Christian my church pushed me to move away from my friends who were like that so I was not tempted to 'return to those ways' (drinking and drugs), as such only in recent years have I reconnected with those people. Whilst the drastic nature of my transformation has an obvious affect on them; 3+years of disconnectedness from me makes a huge barrier."

Loyalty

In my lifetime I have often realised how loyal I am to my friends and family – how patriotic I am towards them and my country too. To say that I would take a bullet for a close friend or family member is an easy thing to do when you haven't got a gun to your head, but more often than not my friends and I would find ourselves in pub-fights sometimes taking the brunt of the action for one another over as little as a pint of beer – spilt by an innocent passerby. Once upon a time in the lower classes of the UK, we would find that a whole community would work in manual jobs in the same place, relying on each other to get a job done, and then taking a break together – playing games and eating with one another.[22] This total reliance on each other for the weekly wage, community, and social interaction would cause relationships to grow closer between workers than between even that of a husband and wife. Communities would, and could, be as loyal to a neighbour as they were to their marriage. The same is true today, the only difference being that in many cases the work is different or non-existent. We still do all of life together, sharing food, space, and social activity. Bennington explains that it is only through this loyalty that the working-class population in Britain were able to come together to increase their quality of living through trade unions because the option was not available for them to do so in the middle-class ways of education, wealth, or social status.[23] To be honest, this whole book is written out of my loyalty and love for my social class, and I think that many of the people reading this book may have felt the same when buying it.

As a Christian with the hidden value of loyalty, you can make a huge difference in the Kingdom of God. Too many people move from church to church because they feel that the '*grass is greener on the other side*,' but God

---

22 Bennington, *Class & Christian Belief*, 38-39.
23 *Ibid*, 38.

needs you to be loyal towards your church and your pastor. Get behind his vision and encourage him or her to be courageous because you will always have their back. Make it clear that you would take a bullet for them. Love them, support them, and encourage your brothers and sisters in Christ to do the same. If the church had more people with this hidden value, it would be unstoppable. Too many pastors have to deal with the stress of backbiting and disloyal congregations, and too many pastors are sent letters about things that they say or do wrong. It saps the fire and vision right out of them, but you can make a huge difference. I love my pastor even though I've moved onto pioneering a church with my family. I still think about him and pray for him all of the time. It makes me angry when he's upset or tired, and it makes me want to drive for over an hour just to do his washing up. Every time that I go home to Northampton I make the point of asking him if there is anything I can do for him. I love him. Your church's mission, and your own ministry, would move so much easier if you let yourself feel the same way.

Relationships

Laura and I first met as teenagers on a council estate in Northampton. Like so many other working-class couples we have been together ever since, despite some difficulties. This ability to put failures and hurts to one side for the sake of our marriage is something that is common among working-class families from across our community. Once again it is worth noting that for chavs, everywhere, people are the most precious possession one can have. This includes your spouse because life would not be the same without them. Your life becomes wrapped up in the life of your spouse, they may be the wage earner in the family, or they may be looking after the children and doing the housework, but to lose such a massive commodity would be like losing life itself. It is a lot like what the bible says about marriage – '*for this reason man will leave his father and mother and will be united to his wife, and the two will become one flesh*' (Mark 10:7-8) – except that for us it was true before we knew God. The people living in biblical times would have known exactly what this means because they too had no other commodities, other than people.

These relationships are able to cope with anything it seems, and no matter what the world throws at us, we just keep on going. I know couples that have been through extreme poverty, adultery, and extreme loss – like that of losing a child – and yet their relationship will not be broken. Their company and unconditional devotion to one another can be seen as comforting, more so than any amount of counselling or psychotherapy – not that we don't need that too. The chances are that this is the same among the middle-class marriages that we see around us, but for me, I am astonished and extremely grateful to my community for showing me what faithfulness means. Even when we have been unfaithful to our spouses, they have remained faithful to us. It's the greatest picture of grace on our estates today.

2 Timothy 2:13 says '*if we are faithless, he remains faithful, for he cannot disown himself*,' when talking about our relationship with Jesus. I believe that a working-class Christian is able to explain, and understand, grace extremely well. We should be encouraged to explore the depths of grace, to study it, and to understand it. Did you know that God would still love you as much as he does right now, even if you were totally against him? What I mean to say is that even if you had never come to follow Jesus, even if no-one on earth had come to follow Jesus, he would have still bled and died for you just in case there was a possibility of you changing your mind – and he would have done it just for you too! As a chav

Christian you should try to get this concept into you, and learn to understand it and practice it. Love those that persecute you, or don't show you justice (Matthew 5:44).

The other thing that a chav Christian can do is to show the world solidarity in marriage. If you're like me, you'll have an awesome amount of jealousy for your wife – so much so that it causes arguments. You can get some great relationship counselling like Laura and I did during college to build trust and help you to communicate well but, until you do, let me advocate for your protection of your marriage. Let me charge you to defend your marriage, no matter what it takes!

Traditions

On our estate, back home, there is a small church over the road from a local pub called The Wheat Sheaf. It isn't by accident that so many of my family have been baptised and married in that church. Working-class people tend to like certain traditions, one of which is getting their children baptised or christened in the local church. When asking people about spirituality recently, a large number of working-class people said that they liked the traditions in church, but didn't understand the teachings. Likewise, since becoming a Christian and for a few years beforehand I was quite interested in going to Midnight

Mass at the Catholic cathedral. This Christmas my sister asked us if we were interested in going to Mass too. She seemed really keen on lighting a candle and taking part in some other traditions.

As a chav Christian maybe you would like to attend the odd traditional service, or to explore some traditions with your friends. There is nothing in the bible to say that you can't take a communion at home with your family. Actually in some churches it is encouraged. The bible offers no specific ways in which traditions should be undertaken. You may find that your friends and family would enjoy taking communion with you on bonfire night, and saying grace before meals would be welcomed in your community. You might like to attend a Catholic Service or go to Mass in a High Anglican church. This can be really fulfilling as you seek to connect with Jesus through lots of different ways. There are also many books about ancient Christian's expressions of faith and spirituality. It would be a good idea to try reading one or two.

Storytelling

All you have to do is walk into a working-class household, grab a brew, and sit down for a chat before you begin to realise the place of storytelling in the chav community. It would be impossible to count the amount of times I've heard the phrase '*did you hear?*'. It is not that the community is full of gossips, although that can be the case sometimes, rather it is just that in our culture we share the news amongst ourselves. Where middle-class people watch the news, or read the newspapers, to catch up on the local and national news; working-class people think on a community level.[24] It's not often that you would find a working-class person reading The Times, or even sitting watching the national news channels that we have on TV. Talking about the news is as much about companionship as it is about information – sometimes more.

Back home culture was built on the stories that we would tell each other. Reputations could be made or broken based on the stories that were bantered around. You would often find that the whole community would know who you are and where you've come from before moving your sofa into the house when moving in. This is great news for the practical and spiritually active Christian, who has the ability to be a good storyteller. The chav Christian is a natural storyteller, who may be able to use humour and exaggerated expressions to give an awesome account of what God is doing in and around the church. This should be harnessed by every church leader. If

24 Payne, *Understanding Poverty*, 59

you're a great storyteller, let me tell you that there are many many stories in the bible that relate to our world today. Study them and learn them off by heart, tell them to your friends and family. When you tell your community about the wonderful things that God is doing, and about your spiritual experiences, your community will be set on fire for God. When I asked a hundred people about church and spirituality, a huge proportion of working-class people said that even if they were not interested in spirituality they would still attend a church if their friends were experiencing the supernatural. Let me tell you that storytelling has been the way to learn and be informed about local news for millennia. Jesus was a storyteller, so be encouraged. Faith comes through hearing (Romans 10:17), which makes your storytelling ability even more important to your local church, and the wider church. I have experienced it so much in my relatively short time in ministry. The more I speak about my God-experiences, the more faith can grow in my church, in my gym, in my home, and in my community.

Before concluding this section of the book let me delve into the wider culture too. We are currently living in a new generation that is known as the postmodern generation. Although there are many things we can learn about ourselves and the people that we live with by studying postmodernism, there is one thing in particular that is relative to our current topic. American Pastor Dan Kimball, when trying to explain postmodernism, tells his readers that the current generation do not believe in an 'absolute truth'. If you could indulge me briefly I will explain a little more. We all have a worldview – this is the basis for everything that you believe. During periods of time there are huge changes in the world that create differing worldviews, for example, during the industrial revolution, society was introduced to scientific theories that made the world lose trust in religion. This gave rise to the worldview that faith and the bible could not be trusted.[25] In the same way in the middle of the twentieth-century there was a pill – meant to stop morning sickness – that had an awful outcome causing birth defects in children.[26] This, in addition to other failings meant that our worldview changed again. Science could not be trusted either. Postmodernism is the conclusion to today's community building a worldview that no longer trusts anything – that is except for experience. With this in mind you can understand the importance of telling stories among your community, as

---

25 D. Kimball, *The Emerging Church: Vintage Christianity for new generations*, (Grand Rapids: Zondervan, 2003), 41-45.

26 The Telegraph, '*Thalidomide: the timeline of scandal,*' http://www.telegraph.co.uk/health/healthnews/9513903/Thalidomide-timeline-of-a-scandal.html, accessed 21st May 2013.

your experience is one of the only things in life that people will trust.

Unemployment

In 1981, the popular reggae band UB40, released a song called *One in Ten* with the lyrics:

> *"I am the one in ten, a number on a list,*
> *I am the one in ten, even though I don't exist,*
> *Nobody knows me, even though I'm always there,*
> *A statistic, a reminder of a world that doesn't care."*

This song was in protest to the unemployment rates of the time, but it seems that unemployment is a characteristic that is attached to the working-class. Although generally society sees this as negative there are some positives. Owen Jones, a writer for the Guardian, explained to his the readers of his book – *Chavs: The demonization of the working class* – that unemployment actually drives down the minimum wage because as long as people are fighting for jobs at the bottom of the ladder; employers are going to be able to push down wages.[27] Jones calls this the 'rat-race to the bottom', and in reality it means that the price of bread stays low, and the services that we use everyday become cheaper. For the rest of society this is good because it lowers inflation

27 Jones, *Chavs*, 202.

and the rich get richer. Ultimately it means that the government do not want 100% employment and so there will never be enough work to go around. However, with this in mind it should be noted that unemployment is not good for the individual because it breeds depression and instability.

In my experience there is no-one that wants to be unemployed. No-one wants to be sitting around all day doing nothing. For the chav Christian this doesn't have to be the case, you have been given a job by the Creator of the universe. Whether you're between jobs, or whether you've been unemployed your whole life, you still have the experience needed to be a real person and a real help to your church and community. Many pastors don't realise it, but they have a workforce that are desperate for something to do just sitting on their doorstep. You could let them know right now by picking up your phone and sending a text. There is plenty of training available in the church, and there is more training available from the government. It would be great for the Kingdom of God if you were to undertake a new course at college or university in an area that you're passionate about, even if you're just going to use it in church. For example, churches need better media, why not contact your local college and ask what you need to do in order to study media, or making films. You could study carpentry or another skill and just help the Kingdom by repairing parts of churches all over your town. The church needs more pastors and there are loads of counselling courses out there – I'm starting one with the Open University in October – and if you're unemployed you can often get on the course at no cost. You can change the world even though you may just be a statistic to the government. You can improve lives, and improve your own by doing so. What's more, with the experience that you get from volunteering around town, you may be offered more work or even end up as your own boss with a tidy little business.

Clothing

When most people hear the word chav, they usually think of hoodies, a cap and Nike trainers. I am one of those people. I love my hats and I'm always told to take them off, whether in a lecture at bible college or preaching in a church. In fact, I've even been asked by members of congregations to take my hat off. In my second year of bible college we had to be part of a church every weekend, performing leadership tasks – from leading a prayer meeting to preaching. At the end of the year our placement supervisor was given a form to fill in about the pupil's performance and ministry. Whilst checking over my form I came across, to me, what was the most insulting question – '*Did the student dress appropriately?*

Let me explain the differences between classes in this respect. Payne claims that in middle-class culture clothing is valued for it's ability to distinguish who is successful. The way in which a middle-class person dresses indicates where they stand in the social ladder, their career, and their quality of life. However, for working-class people clothing is used to show individuality. It is an expression of your personality.[28] It has no influence on how much you are respected, or if you are accepted. Quite often our clothing and fashion is seen as vulgar by those that wish to conform to middle-class standards. Clothing in some areas of working-class life can distinguish between which area you live, and what group you belong to, but ultimately it distinguishes you as a person. A working-class Christian might find it as socially awkward wearing a shirt as he walks down the road, as a middle-class Christian would find wearing her pyjamas to do the school run. What's more, sometimes when I turn up to church I feel like the only person that didn't get the memo saying that the fancy dress party is off.

---

28 Payne, *Understanding Poverty*, 59.

A working-class Christian will be working-class everyday of the week, not ashamed to wear his hat to church, and if aunt Ethel insists on you taking your hat off, just ask her to put hers on. Hallelujah!! Rock that 80's shell-suit and put that diamond earring back in! Ladies slap on your fake tan, and adorn your Uggs and Pat Butcher earrings.

Although some of these values and characteristics may not be our own – as some are attributed to us by society – and some of them may look negative in the light of our capitalist culture, for years we have built traditions, sayings, and behaviours around them. If we look back through history we can see that these values and characteristics when harnessed by the Holy Spirit can be a formidable force as God sweeps through towns, cities, and even countries using the poor or common men and women to do so – just take a look at the Welsh Revival some time. The rest of this book will be looking deeper into particular areas and values of the working-class, and discussing them in more depth. We will also take a look at some of these historic movements of God in England, Scotland, and Wales.

Mannerisms & Etiquette

A writer for The Telegraph, Kate Fox, wrote an article about British etiquette – in fact she wrote a whole book on the subject, *Watching The English.* In her article she wrote:

> "*All English people, whether they admit it or not, are equipped with a highly-sensitive class-radar system – a sort of GPS computer that tells us a person's position on the class map as soon as he or she begins to speak, if not sooner.*"[29]

She goes on to claim that etiquette, in the UK, is used as a social indicator. This is the case even though certain bad manners are used throughout the classes. I would agree with her research and say that there are some habitual behaviours that I wouldn't be seen dead doing – no matter how much you were going to pay me. For example, it took me a good three or four months of

---

29 K. Fox, The Telegraph, '*Everybody's talking about etiquette, but what we're really interested in is class,*' http://www.telegraph.co.uk/comment/personal-view/3618904/Everybodys-talking-about-etiquette-but-what-were-really-interested-in-is-class.html, accessed 23rd May 2013.

attending church to feel comfortable shaking hands with people. At first I thought the church was full of dudes that had a hand-fetish. The only time I would touch a bloke before I was a Christian was to punch him or to act a little camp for jokes. Needless to say that the church, being very middle-class in etiquette, has had plenty of time to sift through middle-class mannerisms and remove those areas that don't fit the Christian faith. In the same way, this chapter will aim to sift through working-class etiquette and mannerisms – not paying too much attention to what middle-class people might call bad manners – to present a working-class Christian etiquette that is both chav and respectful of biblical standards. This should mean that when you're presenting yourself as a Christian, who loves Jesus and reads the bible, you should also be recognised as working-class.

Banter

The Cambridge dictionary describes banter as '*to talk to someone in a friendly and humorous way,*'[30] but I prefer the explanations that you might find on UrbanDictionary.com. Banter is '*Supple term used to describe activities or chat that is playful, intelligent and*

---

30 Cambridge Dictionaries Online, '*Banter,*' http://dictionary.cambridge.org/dictionary/british/banter_2, accessed 24th May 2013.

original. Banter is something you either posses or lack, there is no middle ground. It is also something inherently English, stemming as it does from traditional hi-jinks and tomfoolery of British yesteryear – a word used to cover up what would usually be classed as completely inappropriate behaviour, usually ends in one of the parties being irritated beyond comparison.'[31] A character called Mr Pants once asked the incredibly famous Blackadder "*You're really worked out your banter, haven't you?*" to which Blackadder replied "*No, not really. This is a different thing, it's spontaneous and it's called wit!*"[32] Tim Chester, writer of *Unreached* – a book about ministering to people in urban areas – calls this '*outspoken talk*' and says that middle-class, or 'to do', people tend to find it uncomfortable to be around someone who speaks aggressively.[33]

Ruby Payne claims that in a chav community, personality or character is used for entertainment and that it is highly valued.[34] As someone who likes a bit of banter, and loves to wind people up, I can really relate to this.

---

31 UrbanDictionary, '*Banter,*' http://www.urbandictionary.com/define.php?term=banter, accessed 27th May 2013.

32 Movie Mistakes, '*Blackadder (1986),*' http://www.moviemistakes.com/tv3217/quotes/page2, accessed 27th May 2013.

33 T. Chester, *Unreached*, 68.

34 Payne, *Understanding Poverty*, 59.

Every time that I go home I have to battle through a good five minutes of abuse from each family member that I see before we can settle into a normal conversation. I love it though. In the same way, if you are a working-class Christian, I would recommend keeping and practicing this skill. This ability to speak with confidence and wit – thinking quickly on the spot with a little pressure – can be harnessed and used for preaching and teaching. Believe it or not, when middle-class people get used to your humour, they begin to like it too, and this confidence in speaking is highly desirable. Another way in which your confidence in speaking can be used is in outreach opportunities. Once again, your cultural relevance is brilliant for reaching the world for Jesus. Why not join a gym or some sort of sports club. People will love you for your character, and will respect you for your faith. Use and abuse your talent for Jesus.

A theme that I will introduce throughout this book from now on is respect. If you are going to tell jokes and have a laugh, or if you are going to deliberately insult people, you must remember that this works so well on our estates because everyone is so close. These jokes and abuse can only be used with people that you have a close relationship with. You must also remember to respect people's feelings and insecurities when having this sort of conversation. God loves people, and sometimes we need to remember that the person we may be speaking about is God's daughter and he loves her – or God's son.

Sexuality

Working-class hero, and footballer, Paul Gascoigne wrote about his experience as a child growing up in a council home with his siblings. Whilst doing so he candidly recalls a story involving his sister Anna:

> *"Anna was the talented one, great at singing and dancing, and we used to put on little shows for the neighbours, entrance 2p. She would sing and dance and I would rush in and do a striptease, which infuriated her because she took it very seriously."*[35]

Gazza, like many of his working-class counterparts, is not shy about sexual matters. For me, growing up around people that were open about sexual matters was normal. As much as banter consists of humorous and witty insults, as soon as my friends felt comfortable, or sometimes sooner, they would be some of the crudest people I've ever heard. It seems like the words used during such conversations were meant to be a shock. The shock itself is the comedy in the conversation. During

35 P. Gascoigne & H. Davies, *Gazza: My story*, (London: Headline Book Publishing, 2004), 14.

my time at bible college I decided to have some counselling – as it was free, why not use it? Part of my counselling in my third year of college was to help me figure out why I wanted to shock everyone. It turns out that by doing this, upon entering a room full of people, I take control of the room. This was my way of levelling the playing field in a place where I felt uncomfortable. This could be the case for many other people, but I think the main reason sexuality is more open amongst the working-class is simply because we don't have to structure the things we talk about to gain spaces on the social ladder. We don't care about moving up the social ladder after all. Therefore, in our culture, sexuality is not something that we need to keep a secret, so a chav Christian would naturally be as open about sexuality – sometimes even using it for comedic value – as their friends and family do.

It is important at this point – before every middle-class Christian reading this starts to bring objections – to mention that the bible itself speaks quite openly about sexuality. The Song of Songs is extremely candid on the subject, with some of the language used in the book even being a little vulgar for my innocent eyes. It is believed that Jewish men were not allowed to read the book until they were thirty years old.[36] It might just be me, but it looks like the 'privatisation' of sexuality might have been another Conservative move rather than a biblical one. Although I joke, it is paramount that I once again express my concern for respect. It's one thing to add a little euphemism into your sentence or an innuendo, but it's another thing to disrespect someone's sister, mother, or your own wife. The Message version of the bible says: "Watch the way you talk. Let nothing foul or dirty come out of your mouth" (Ephesians 4:29). Where a cleverly placed innuendo can liven up a room, a misplaced cuss can kill a relationship. It's important that we gather some perspective on social-awareness. Nowadays I tend not to talk in this manner at all, although sometimes when I'm with my close friends someone might let an innuendo slip. In fact, I won some respect for Jesus a little while ago when a not-yet-Christian friend suggested something about my wife, and I was strong enough to rebuke him gently by just reminding him that I love my wife. I pray with all my heart that you might learn to be the best Christian, before trying to be the best chav Christian.

---

36 J. D. Baildam, *Paradisal Love: Johann Gottfried Herder and the Song of Songs*, (Sheffield: Sheffield Academic Press, 1999), 146.

Toilet Humour

Toilet humour has always been a very British form of comedy.[37] San Francisco University lecturer, Arthur Berger, explains:

> *"Comedians have told me that sometimes they have to adapt their humor and if cerebral humor or routines based on allusions and word play, for instance, aren't going over with a working-class audience, a shift to toilet humor is often effective."*[38]

The second shop that I managed, before becoming a Christian, was a flooring store just on the edge of our estate. My first day on the job a trader named Simon came in to check out the new manager. Simon was, and is, the epitome of a working-class bloke. As he entered my shop he stubbed out his cigarette just outside the door and continued to walk past my counter – letting go of one of the largest, and stinkiest, farts I've ever heard or smelt in my life. Quietly chuckling to himself he acted like nothing had happened and began to explain which

---

37 For comedic value, check out the fun and artistic toilet ornament designed by Colin Painter; Sarah Lucas, Victoria and Albert Museum, '*Close Encounters of the Art Kind: The old in out (saggy version),*' http://www.vam.ac.uk/content/articles/c/close-encounter-the-old-in-out-saggy-version-sarah-lucas/, accessed 25th May 2013.

38 A. A. Berger, *Blind Men And Elephants: Perspectives on humor*, (New Brunswick: Transaction Publishers, 1995), 30.

sort of door one of his customers needed, telling me about his cooked breakfast on the way. Over the next four years managing flooring shops we would laugh and joke about his ice-breaker as we became good friends.

In the same way in which working-class people aren't all that bothered about keeping their sexuality private, they are not really bothered about keeping their bodily expulsions private either. This is just another way of breaking the awkwardness in a room or environment that might be a little tough. If you want to make a chav feel welcome, just let one rip in his presence. When Laura and I first got together, Laura opened the door to toilet humour in our relationship by belching in my face. Quite often you will hear a naughty little chav in our household say that they laughed so much they wee'd a little bit. It doesn't matter if you're aspiring working-class or just plain happy to be in your council house working-class, there's no way that you can hold it together when someone starts cracking them out. This is part of your culture, don't be shy about it. In normal fashion, however, let me be quick to point out that we need to be an ambassador for Jesus, not just our culture, and so when it comes to having manners in an environment outside of your house, try to be civilised for the sake of mission amongst middle-class culture and try to be a good representative for working-class Christians amongst your fellow church folk.

Dress-Code

My college lecturer and pastor for three years, Pete Read, once told me that I don't know how to do smart-casual. He said that I can do casual and I can do smart, but I can't do smart-casual. This was at a wedding where most of the people who knew me there, said that they had to take a second glance at me because they didn't recognise me. Working-class people love to dress up for a wedding or special occasion, and love to dress comfortably the rest of the time. This would be because, like I mentioned earlier, we don't use our clothes in the same way that middle-class people do. There's nothing wrong with middle-class people dressing the way they do, and there's nothing wrong with them jockeying for position on the social ladder, but working-class people just don't feel the same way about life and aspirations. This means that some people may take offence at the way we dress. As I have already mentioned in this book however, we should be allowed to be working-class and that means keeping our working-class etiquette when it comes to clothing.

I'm sure you already know when it is really necessary to dress appropriately, for example weddings and funerals, but the rest of the time just feel free to be a chav Christian and dress how you want. I love wearing my socially-unacceptable socks and sandals around, and I love to wear my cap at church. Believe it or not, God is actually able to reach down to you through your hat and speak to you despite the way you dress. I urge you to be you!!

Table Etiquette

Kate Fox, who I mentioned earlier, uses the way that we eat peas at the dinner table – *pea etiquette* – to show the basic difference between classes when it comes to eating. She wrote:

> *"The etiquette books' "correct" method of eating peas (i.e. the middle/upper-class method) is to use your knife to squash the peas onto the convex back of the fork. The "incorrect" (working-class) method is to turn the fork prongs-up and scoop peas up with it, as though it were a spoon. The incorrect method is clearly more sensible, or at least more ergonomic, in that more peas per forkful are transported from plate to mouth - about 13 on average, according to my tests, as*

opposed to about eight using the socially superior squashing method."[39]

Let's face it, when I'm eating my fish and chips, I couldn't care less what people think about the way I eat, I just want to cram it. If picking up chips with my fingers is a sign of poverty, then I'm glad to be poor. I didn't know what a spork was until I was about thirteen years old, and never went to a restaurant until I moved in with my grandparents. Growing up, living with my mum, the only time I saw a table was when we went to the pub or Maccy D's. Ruby Payne tells her readers that, for the working-class, food is a matter of survival. We're not bothered about the correct way to eat, we just know that we have to eat in order to live. The quality of the food doesn't have to be important, merely making sure there is enough is the most important thing.[40]

This means that when people invite myself, and other working-class people to their homes, the first thing that comes into our head is '*I don't want to embarrass myself at the table.*' What's more, '*I can't keep up with my hosts style of living, and so couldn't invite them back to mine for dinner.*'

---

39 K. Fox, The Telegraph, '*Everybody's talking about etiquette, but what we're really interested in is class,*' http://www.telegraph.co.uk/comment/personal-view/3618904/Everybodys-talking-about-etiquette-but-what-were-really-interested-in-is-class.html, accessed 23rd May 2013.

40 Payne, *Understanding Poverty*, 59.

This means that when someone from church invites us round for a meal, our response will most likely be one of refusal. The best way to invite your working-class Christian friend round for dinner is to invite them round for a general chat quite close to a meal time, and then whilst chatting explain to them that dinner is almost ready and there is enough to go around. I love to eat, and I love to be myself. This means that the people around me have to deal with my unorthodox behaviour or stop inviting me round. If you're one of my many Facebook friends you will notice that I often post pictures of myself cramming food into my mush. What used to be a sign of defiance in the face of my middle-class colleagues and friends has now turned into fun saga of food thuggery. Don't be ashamed to be yourself. Your friends and colleagues from church just want to spend time with you, they are not bothered about how you eat and, if I'm honest, they would probably enjoy experimenting with your cultural differences. Some of my best friends are foreign, and I love their food and their table manners. I love the quirky little things they do. I love the fact that my North-Indian next door neighbour used to bring me lamb curry with bones in it round to my house for me to eat. In their household everyone sat on the sofas, and if a man had nowhere to sit a woman would have to give up their seat for him. I love it. I love seeing new things, and trying new things. What's more, so do many other people. Your friends will love you more for being yourself, than what they ever will for trying to be posh. Eat like a chav enit.

Aggression

The Victorian saying '*children should be seen and not heard*' is a common saying within the walls of a working-class house. Many people from my background can probably remember their parents, certainly their dad, being rather authoritarian.[41] Most of us actually grow up in a sort of hostile environment, not just in home but at school and when we're out playing football or tag in the park too. Aggression is just a normal part of life for a working-class person, and if you don't learn to be aggressive at the right times you'll be taken for a mug. When writing about the first time he had met Vinnie Jones, Gazza wrote:

> *"It's quite normal for more experienced players to try to intimidate you, sometimes by threatening to kill or maim you, especially if you're young and new or seen as a fancy-dan player. But one look at Vinnie and I believed his*

---

41 K. Marjoribanks, *Family and School Capital: Towards a context theory of students' school outcomes*, (Norwell: Kluwer Academic Publishers, 2002), 140.

threat. I didn't think he was acting, though we know now what a good actor he has become. I was sure he meant it, and I was right."[42]

Gazza then went on, in his autobiography, to explain about the world-famous picture of Vinnie Jones grabbing and squeezing his genitals. Although this is a funny story, aggression and straight talking are just a normal part of life for us. Tim Chester tells his readers that in his experience, working-class people prefer it if you just tell them straight, even if it means being honest about the fact that they are destined for hell.[43] The truth is that as a working-class Christian, you and I will sometimes have to hold back our words and feelings in order to keep the peace with our middle-class neighbours. However, there will be times when truth is truth and to be kind to our brothers and sisters we may have to hurt them. Just try to put a bit of sugar in the medicine. Advice is best given as a positive rather than a negative. For example, rather than saying "*I think your work was crap because...*" why not try saying something along the lines of "*such and such a thing might have improved your work and made it more accessible...*" There is another old saying that would do you right in any of these situations – "*if you're not going to say anything nice, then don't say it at all.*"

---

42 Gascoigne & Davies, *Gazza*, 73.
43 Chester, *Unreached*, 68.

Hospitality

Living in a bible college environment for the past three years has been a bit of a culture-shock. One of the main things that I've noticed is that my friends actually knock on the door when they come round. Back home a member of the family's home is almost like your own. I would always have friends that would come round and help themselves to my tools or lawnmower from my garden, or they would feel welcome to walk in my front door. It is only after three years with my colleagues at bible college that some of them have started walking in without knocking.

An open house is part and parcel of being working-class. A friend of mine, Carl Belcher an Eden Network regional leader, once told me that having an open home is one of the most important things about being an Eden volunteer. The Eden Network are a great Christian missionary organisation that work with people living in deprived areas in the UK. They know from experience, just as I know from living in a working-class culture, that we don't make dinner dates or appointments – we just turn up, often not even knocking and expect a cup of tea at a whim.

This is a great way of living, if we look at Jesus and Zacchaeus (Luke 19:1-10) we can see how Jesus turns into a right chav for a few hours as he approaches the tax collector – who, by the way, would have been a social outcast, the lowest of low. David Cameron would have called him the Jewish feral underclass – Jesus commands him: "*get down from that tree and cook me some dinner at your house.*" In the same way that my chav brothers and sisters won't be too keen on going to a dinner party round someone's house, they might be forward enough to demand dinner at a whim. If you're a middle-class pastor or house-group leader and your chav Christian friend does this, take it as a compliment, they like you!! If you're a working-class Christian who is as outgoing as me, most middle-class people actually like you too, and would love for you to eat with them. The chances are that they have been wondering if you'll eat with them for a while. Just make the first move, and be a chav.

You may disagree with some of the things that I've said in this chapter, and that's fine – I was wrong once too. Etiquette is the very concept that distinguishes class in the street. What you think are bad manners are actually a part of culture. For example, many foreign people don't queue in their countries, and so they have no problem with jumping a queue in our country. To them pushing to the front of a queue is the cultural norm, but for us it is bang out of order. There are many behaviours in middle-class etiquette that chavs find offensive, and vice-versa. We just need to accept each other for who we are. The gospel should transcend class, race, culture, and etiquette. Let's make it happen.

Justice

I'm not sure that any amount of writing can help us comprehend fully the concept of justice. Neither do I believe that this is the right time for me to enter into a rant regarding politics, and how working-class people may feel that they have been dealt an injustice by those that have the most influence in our nation. Instead I will attempt to explore God's justice, and try to bring some understanding in relation to justice and love.

If you're a pastor or missionary aiming at reaching out to Britain's working-class communities, I would say that the best way in which you can begin to bring justice to our community is by understanding our aspirations. After all, if you can get your thoughts beyond middle-class aspirations and try to understand working-class aspirations – this means accepting that they are legitimate goals – then you will be able to understand why we have the opinions that we do. For example, getting a temporary job in telesales – one of the very few options currently available at the bottom of the career ladder – means signing off from benefits with the risk of being fired after a couple of weeks due to a current lack of employee rights in the workplace. This in turn means the hassle of reapplying for benefits with long delays, racking up more debt and risking being evicted from your lifelong home. It is easy to see why many people just will not turn up for interviews or try to get a job. What's more the minimum wage leaves many people out of pocket and relying on tax credits to cover their living costs. Justice in this case would not just mean fighting for the rights of employees, but it would also mean accepting the logic of the person that doesn't want to be treated like a slave for two weeks in order to be refused benefits and get evicted from their home. If you would like to know more about this sort of concept, you will have to read a lot more books as this book does not have the space to speak about it. This book is about mentoring working-class people on their spiritual journey – as a working-class Christian. With this in mind we'll carry on.

Inclusivity

Whilst working-class aspirations are still fresh in our mind, it is worth noting once again that people are our biggest commodity. Without our community, friends, and family we wouldn't be able to live as comfortably as we do. Despite what the papers and government would like you to believe, working-class people are not racist by nature. The papers tell us that foreign people take our jobs and our houses, but in reality we know that, for those of us that work, no-one is taking our jobs. We also know that the reason for the shortage in housing is Thatcher's attempt to make us homeless, and the proceeding governments lack of vision and insight.

My nan always tells me about her next door neighbours, who were an Indian family, and how they would invite her round for dinner – never forgetting to mention the fish heads in her curry. When we were back in Spencer our next door neighbours were from northern India and they would treat us in the same way. Quite often I would get a knock at the door and my neighbour would be standing there with her kids holding dishes full of curry, rice, and homemade sweets. I remember the joy on the kids faces when I would take round a trifle or chocolate cake. It seems that my Indian neighbours knew more about living in an impoverished community than most of the writers I see on the bookshelves writing about community. In the same manner, most working-class communities welcome anyone with open arms and are quick to include people in their new community. This myth about working-class people being racist was one of UB40's other passions. During the race riots of the 80's this band deliberately included multiple ethnicities from their own community into their band in order to bring unity.[44]

As a working-class Christian you will know the importance of feeling welcome. Your skills of hospitality are amazing because they have been taught to you for your whole life. It would be great for you to use this gift in church, helping accidental cliques to become inclusive and serving on the welcome and hospitality teams at church. After all, the most important job in church is hospitality.

Pain & Suffering

If I had a pound for every time that I heard an 'uber-Christian' say something along the lines of '*there is no promise of happiness for people that choose to follow Jesus*' I would be minted. Here's the thing though, I have never been happier than I am now. It's not because I have material wealth, or even a fulfilling job. I might say that I understand emotions and love now, and that this has caused me to live a happier life, and a more fulfilled marriage. I'm sure there are lots of Christians that can say the same too. However, I and so many other working-

---

44 UB40: The Official Site, '*The History: Introduction,*' http://www.ub40.co.uk/introduction.html, accessed 31st May 2013.

class people know how deep pain and suffering can go. It's not that we suffer more than middle-class people, but it may be the case that suffering is a way of life for the average working-class individual.

Many of you might feel like me – in that I'm not all that bothered about what the world has to throw at me because I've been through enough hardship to learn that 'life goes on'. I hear many Christians, that don't have a clue what we go through, saying things like '*just put on a brave face*' or '*God has a plan for your suffering*'. All of these sayings and proverbs make me angry. There's nothing wrong with admitting that we're suffering, and to put on a brave face or try to praise through your suffering often belittles your pain. In recent times I've read some books written by some amazing authors. For example, C. S. Lewis – the writer of Narnia – writes quite candidly about pain and suffering. One of my favourite books of his is called *A Grief Observed*, in which he writes about his emotions after his wife's death. It is incredibly moving how he takes his readers on a journey of questioning his friends motives, and then even questioning God.[45] It can often seem like God isn't near when we're hurting, but

---

45 C. S. Lewis, *A Grief Observed*, (London: Faber & Faber Ltd, 1961), 49.

the experiences shared in these books bring God to life through our suffering.

As working-class Christians often will have lived a lifestyle of suffering, it is possible that you will be able to have incredible empathy with people that are going through pain. I once started reading a book titled *Let The Healing Begin* by Jeannie Morgan, and within the first couple of chapters I was broken to pieces, barely holding the tears back as I just seemed to feel every emotion going through her body. In her first chapter she tells of her aspiration to have children. It almost felt like her life was empty and worthless if she could not conceive. Unfortunately, try as she would, it seemed like her life's ambition was not going to happen, until one day she fell pregnant. She explains so many of her feelings and as I was reading I was getting sucked in by a barrage of different emotions. Within a short time she fell pregnant again with her second child. One day as she was answering a knock at the door, clutching her baby girl in her arms, her older daughter – now a toddler – fell into her swimming pool and drowned. She recalls the story:

> *"We thought she was upstairs, but as Alex and I reached the half-landing and looked outside, we saw Joanna floating in the pool."*[46]

It was at this point in the story that I think my heart stopped beating and I had to grab a tissue. You as a Christian would be feeling like someone had wrenched your heart from your chest and stamped on it at this point, as your friend told you a story of suffering like this, and you as a working-class Christian know of many struggles and pain. You can handle this pain well. As a chav Christian you have the gift of empathy and compassion. I suggest you use it well. We don't have space in this book to tell you the ins and outs of counselling and pastoral care, so I will try to help you a little with some words of wisdom from one of my favourite writers – Paul Tournier.

Paul Tournier is a medical doctor, and a Christian, who is famous for making a link between spiritual wellbeing and physical health. He claims that by giving his patients some extra time to talk about their problems, and what's going on in life, they tend to recover quicker and get ill less often.[47] It is not how well you talk to people, but how

---

46 J. Morgan, *Let The Healing Begin*, (Eastbourne: David C Cook, 2007), 21.

47 P. Tournier, *A Listening Ear*, (London: Hodder & Stoughton, 1984).

well you listen. Tournier said that in order to practice listening properly he would try to relay what he thought his patient, or wife, was saying back to them. This would also let them know that he was listening.[48] Tournier expresses his understanding of the way in which men and women communicate by explaining that men are more mechanical in their thinking, whereas women are more technical. This means that men work out problems with a scientific objective mind, but women are theoretical and relational in their thinking. However, he tells his readers that in recent years women have adapted so that they can understand male social psychology. This leaves men emotionally-handicapped – thus making them socially-handicapped. I would say that this isn't so for our postmodern chav culture today however. If you want to be an effective chav Christian you will need to let your emotions out, and seek understanding in regards to what they are. Let your passion and compassion be freed into the world that seeks a listening ear.

Derek Talbot, one of the visiting lecturers at Regents Theological College, told our class about how important it is to listen. Derek takes funerals as a full-time job and reads lots of books in his spare time. He is the person that introduced me to reading Paul Tournier's books.

---

48 Tournier, *A Listening Ear*, 67-75.

Derek taught that when someone is going through the grieving process, they often need to tell their story over and over again in order for it to sink in. Telling their story is their way of finding comfort and reliving a moment in life that changed everything. The people around you that are suffering and telling you their story are not looking for advice on how to get over it, or move on, they just need to tell you their story. All you have to do, in order to make their world a better place, is listen to that story.

Guilt

It wasn't long after becoming a Christian that I started to realise to what extent guilt could affect our lives. One day I was sitting in a counselling session when I was asked "*What words make you feel emotional?*" My answer took a little while, but I started with my wife and my kids, before moving onto my granddad, and then slowly I began to say the words 'guilt' and 'shame'. As I said "*shame*" my heart sank and I began to cry a little. This is a normal feeling for anyone that has realised that they the things that they do wrong hurt the most important person in their life. The pain that I had caused Jesus was now beginning to cause me emotional pain.

Smith Wigglesworth was, and still is, one of the world's most well known healing evangelists. His ministry to the sick and hurting was so successful that when he met up with a friend of his at a funeral, he proceeded to ask him whether the daughter that Smith had recently prayed for had been healed. To Smith's surprise the young girl had not. At hearing this he suddenly began to convulse before dying on the very spot.[49] Up until this point Wigglesworth had been your typical working-class Christian. He began his adulthood working in the wool mills in Bradford, and soon met a man who taught him about the bible at the same time as teaching him about plumbing. Soon enough he began his spiritual walk and began trying to serve the church evangelistically.[50] Smith went on for about fourteen years trying his hardest to live a godly life, and serve God with his evangelistic fervour. The first years of being married to his wife, Polly, were blissful and happy as they started their own missional hub called the Bowland Street Mission. Polly would preach and Smith would look after the children, bringing people in off the street.[51] At this point in his ministry Smith could barely string two words together, and he couldn't really read either. Before long his

---

49 J. Wilson, *Wigglesworth: the complete story*, (Milton Keynes: Authentic Media, 2002), 5-6.

50 *Ibid*, 11-12.

51 *Ibid*, 28.

plumbing business would almost destroy his faith as he became extremely busy and his spiritual life began to suffer. He would often have arguments at home and was quite brash towards his wife. Eventually though, he began to seek God again as Polly began praying for him. Wigglesworth said:

> "*I can remember a time when I used to go white with rage and shake all over with temper. I could hardly hold myself together. I waited on God for ten days. In those ten days, I was being emptied out and the life of the Lord Jesus Christ was being wrought in me. My wife testified of the transformation that took place in my life. "I never saw such a change," my wife said. "I have never been able to cook anything since that time that has not pleased him. Nothing is too hot or cold, everything is just right.*"[52]

Smith's transformation had been brought on by what Pentecostals call *the baptism of the Spirit*, and it wasn't only noticed by his wife. Some of his employees approached him after noticing the difference, asking "*We would like that spirit you have.*"

---

52 *Ibid*, 29-30.

The reason for this holiness in Smith Wigglesworth's life, and in our own, is that when we are born again spiritually the new spirit that we have has the desires and values of God. It is almost like we now have the DNA of God. The bible says that if we are born again of God's Spirit we cannot go on sinning (1 John 3:9). If you're anything like me you will know the pain and heartache that sin can cause in the world, and so you will be so against it that you might accidentally become very legalistic – this means that you will try to force your friends and family to keep the laws of God. However, you must remember that those around you are responsible for themselves. The only person that you are responsible for is yourself. It took me a long time to realise this, and I've burnt a lot of bridges – having friends fall out with me – and I wouldn't want you to do the same. One of the most graceful things that you can do in life is take onboard the teaching and experience of others. This is one of those times. Pray for understanding in regards to the baptism of the Spirit, grace, and holiness.

With your new DNA you will also have a heightened passion to see justice fulfilled. This means that you'll be even more concerned with seeing people treated fairly, and given the respect that they deserve, than you ever have. As a chav Christian you're not going to stand for injustice like the average person. You will want to do something about it. I'll just repeat that: you will want to *DO* something about it!!! And that's awesome. Do it! Find out how you can do it, apply to do it, and then do it. When you see a homeless dude sitting at the side of the street give him your last £10. Working-class people are more inclined to give without asking questions. Who cares what he spends it on? Don't judge that person before you know them. Just give! I remember once when I slept on a bench at the side of the road for three days when I was 16 years of age. The only way I was going to get home was if someone gave me £40, but because people thought I was going to spend the money on drink or drugs I had to sleep on a bench for three days. I ended up borrowing someone's phone to ring a relative to pick me up. Just give!

Holiness

One of Smith Wigglesworth's greatest desires was to become holy and he's not the only working-class hero of the faith to feel the same way. From what I read in history books and biographies, it seems like the default position of a working-class christian is the thought: *I would do anything to be holy because I want to get as close to Jesus as possible.* This desire for holiness, in my own life, seems to stem from two areas. The first being, if I'm holy

I will not hurt Jesus or other people. This means that your holiness, and my own, springs from a desire to see people treated fairly and with respect. My holiness comes from a sense of justice then. Secondly, my holiness comes from the Holy Spirit of God living with me, changing my desires to match his. If God truly lives in me like the bible says that he does, then the results will be the same. For example, in Acts 4 we see the Spirit filled believers going against the beliefs and practices of the day by selling everything they had to make sure that everyone had enough to live. In my third year of bible college I did a module of Christian leadership. As part of this module our class undertook a personality test, known as the *Strength Finder*. One of the strengths that was mentioned in this test was called *Belief.* This concept of belief meant that any person possessing this strength would have a determination to defend what he or she believes is right. Often quite vocal, if needed, this person will defend justice with everything they have, even if it means upsetting people around them, and maybe even losing friends.[53] This is chav behaviour. Needless to say that I have this strength. I just cannot sit back and let injustice prevail. I have to say something or do something, and so do you. That is fine, but remember once again that you

---

53 M. Buckingham & D. O. Clifton, *Now, Discover Your Strengths: How to develop your talents and those of the people you manage*, (London: Pocket Books, 2004), 82-83.

are a chav Christian. Try to respect the fact that you may not know everything, and that the person who is committing an injustice may not have been educated to a point of understanding what they are doing. God loves people, and so should you!

Another part of this holiness and determination to do what is right, no matter what, is that you will aim to be holy even if it is going against the grain of the culture that you are part of. This shouldn't be a problem because you are used to being part of a sub-culture that doesn't conform to the rest of the world. I want to encourage you to be a sub-culture in Christian life too. Be holy no matter what comes against you. Go against the grain of apathy in our churches today. Be like John Wesley who would get kicked out of Anglican churches for preaching holiness and sanctification as a gift from the Holy Spirit.[54] Let's make chav Christianity a sub-culture of holiness in the church of God today.

Possessed By God's Spirit

One of my favourite scriptures is Isaiah 61, which reads:

> *"The Spirit of the Sovereign Lord is on me,*
> *because the Lord has anointed me to preach good*

---

54. R. Hattersly, John Wesley: A brand from the burning, (London: Time Warner Books UK, 2002), 74-75.

news to the poor. He has sent me to bind up the brokenhearted, to proclaim freedom for the captives and release from darkness for the prisoners, to proclaim the year of the Lord's favor and the day of vengeance of our God, to comfort all who mourn, and provide for those who grieve in Zion – to bestow on them a crown of beauty instead of ashes, the oil of gladness, instead of mourning, and a garment of praise instead of a spirit of despair."

This was one of the first scriptures that Jesus read in a public setting and, as a man, this is one of the most inspiring and moving scriptures at my disposal. Every good thing that we do, and everything powerful thing that we do should come from our relationship with God. That relationship is based on our willingness to be slaves to God, and his Spirit that lives in us. In order for us to be holy, we need to invite Holy to live within us, to transform us.

Before heading off to bible college I used to work for a Christian charity in Northampton, called Spencer Contact. Every Thursday we would have a prayer meeting for one hour. As I began to draw closer to God, and as he showed himself to me on a more personal level, I found myself calling out to him for a deeper love for people. On one occasion in our Thursday prayer meeting, I asked God with every ounce of sincerity to "*show me the way that you feel about people, and give me a taste of the love that you have for your people.*" After all if I was going to win people for Jesus, I needed to know how Jesus felt about them so that I could speak from truth and experience, rather than blind faith. The following Monday my wife and I were shopping in Morrison's when, as I was walking up the isle, a man stood in front of me looking at some groceries. A rush of emotions hit me as I began to feel God's love for this man, and I began to cry as God told me that this man may not make it into heaven and eternal life. My wife, in shock and horror, quickly reminded me that we were shopping and that it isn't good for men to cry in public. The same thing happened again in the next isle and I had to keep my head down for the whole time that we were shopping. The following night we were eating dinner with the children, when I saw an NHS advert on the TV. It is worth noting now that I am very keen on food – I love to eat!! This advert featured a painter-decorator who was painting on some scaffolding, and as he stepped back to look at his work, he fell over and smashed into a million pieces, like glass, on the floor. At this sight, I felt the same emotions as I did when shopping and had to stop eating my food and hold back the tears. This intensely spiritual experience of love lasted nearly two weeks as I lost a little weight and became frustrated with every Christian that I knew because they were letting their friends, family, neighbours, colleagues, and the world be lost to the enemy. As I learned to control these intense emotions I sat in the presence of my colleagues, and my elder, and asked God for a double helping! Needless to say that my elder quickly stepped in and insisted that I couldn't handle that sort of pain, and urged me to reconsider my prayer. This experience was so real, not just to me but to all of the people that I lived and worked with for those two weeks too.

The point of my story is this: You will not know what true justice is until you have been filled and possessed by God's Holy Spirit!! I am, by nature, a sceptical abrupt and dismissive introvert, but with God in me and by giving everything that I am over to him to change this world I am known as a man of faith, love, peace, and joy. Hallelujah!!

Lifestyle

Working-class people, like other cultures and sub-cultures that are generally lower in the social order, tend to be rather resourceful. This has been proven in many ways. Take for example a single-parent recently featured in the Guardian newspaper. Jackie Monroe, after losing nearly £100 a month from her housing benefit, had to learn to feed herself and her young son on just £10 a week. Jackie began to write a blog about her struggles and the things that she would sell, and have to give up, in order just to live.[55] The resourcefulness of the poor is just one aspect of our lifestyle that stands out in working-class culture. The fact that we have less, in terms of material wealth, determines much of our lifestyle choices. What's more, due to our aspirations and values, we tend to live a lifestyle that fits our general group even if we have plenty of capital. Take for example the local working men's club. Quite often you might find that certain members of the community might like to think of themselves as slightly more plush

---

55 P. Butler, The Guardian, '*Jack Monroe: the face of modern poverty*', http://www.guardian.co.uk/society/2013/jul/23/jack-monroe-face-modern-poverty?CMP=twt_gu, accessed 25th July 2013.

than other members, these will often supply their not so plush neighbours with beers for the evening. I can remember many occasions whilst growing up, friends and family would buy my beers before payday without even thinking about asking for a beer in return once I had been paid. Their salary might have been able to last the fortnight even if they did buy a couple of extra beers, whilst mine barely lasted me the week. With that sort of mentality in mind this chapter will look at the lifestyle of those that belong to working-class culture, and aim to inspire you with ways of encouraging community and friendship with your working-class neighbour.

Dinner Dates

If you're a Christian, that has had trouble reaching out to your working-class friends, the chances are that even if you began your spiritual journey as a working-class person you no longer are. This would be because most people conform to the dominant culture that they are surrounded by. As a middle-class Christian you probably invite people round for dinner and you might be wondering why your working-class neighbour or friend won't have dinner with you. If this is the case with you, then there's good news in store. I'm going to try to help you.

Working-class people don't like to eat at another persons expense without having had them eat at their own expense. If they haven't brought you dinner before there's not much chance of them letting you buy them dinner. Many working-class people would also think that they can't compete with your style of eating either. Another distinction between working-class people and middle-class people is this: when thinking about food or buying food, working-class people think about quantity because the most important question in their mind is 'do I have enough to feed my family?' Whereas the middle-class person tends to think in terms of quality. They don't have to worry about money, or food running out, because they may have slightly higher income or savings. So when a working-class person looks at a middle-class person's invite to dinner, they are thinking either 'can I afford to eat out with them?' or 'can I compete with their hospitality and will I like their posh food?'. Nine times out of ten you may well get rejected by your friend or colleague if they are working-class. However, there are some ways to break down these barriers. Firstly, when inviting your chav friend round for dinner, don't call it dinner. Ask them if they can come round to help with something or to have a cuppa. Once they are in the house you can very easily explain that you'll be having food soon and that you've cooked enough for everyone. If they still argue back, just tell them that you wouldn't want to waste it. Secondly, go to their home. It pains me to see so many working-class families neglected by middle-class church folk, mainly because they might feel uncomfortable on a particular estate, or in a certain environment. If you're scared of the area, just remember that your working-class friend would probably take a bullet for you. Literally!! Once you've started going into their home often enough, it's just a matter of time until they invite you to eat and drink with them. Then you're in. After a couple of meals you may well be able to buy them lunch in a decent pub somewhere. The third option is to go round on a Friday evening and wait until it's time to order a kebab or pizza. This way you can pay for your own food and they'll pay for their own and everyone will be happy.

If you're working-class, my message is basic for you. These lovely Christian folks aren't interested in what you can give back. They just want to bless you. It took me two years of being a Christian to realise that it was ok to take something without having to give something. Happy eating!!

Coffee Shops

As I've already mentioned, working-class people put quality quite low on their list of needs. So it is ridiculous to even consider consuming coffee in a shop like Starbucks or Costa – specially when we have Nescafe at home. I can understand that many people like the atmosphere in coffee shops because of the type of people that they attract, but if you're inviting your working-class friend out, you're more likely to get them into a local cafe or a pub. The atmosphere in the local pub or cafe may be slightly more intimidating for people that aren't used to it, but part of the reason for that intimidation is the exact reason that we like to spend time there. The local cafe and pub will have a set of regulars that all know each other quite well. When you walk into that place you are walking into a community that could have been established over generations. The difference in your middle-class coffee shop is that there is no community. It is just an atmosphere that holds within it lots of different conversations and friendships. The beauty about going into a local pub or cafe on a regular basis is that you soon become part of that community. If you're going to win these people for Jesus you will need to learn about networks and what they mean to postmodern Britain. If I may, I would like to tell all of my working-class colleagues that, even if they stop drinking when they become a Christian, it is still good to keep in touch with those networks that you are part of. If you love your community and friends then you will want them to experience the awesome power of God, and his grace, too. It is possible to be on a darts team and be a Christian. Likewise, it is possible to claim benefits and be a Christian, after all even Jesus claimed benefits when he was caught gleaning on the Sabbath (Mark 2:23). In the Old Testament God made a law stating that farmers should not go right to the edges of their fields when harvesting. This was so that poor people could come behind them and pick (glean) any leftovers. This was the earliest form of a welfare system. So even Jesus claimed benefits. Whatever happens though, try to keep in touch with your community and friends. As a chav Christian you should be putting them before anybody else. Playing golf and drinking Costa Coffee isn't something that Christians are called to do, it is just part of the culture that the majority of Christians belong to.

Carrot Sticks

Have you ever noticed how obsessed with health the majority of middle-class people are? I have noticed it on a very large scale ever since becoming a Christian. Most Christians quote 1 Corinthians 6:19: "*Do you not know that your bodies are temples of the Holy Spirit, who is in you, whom you have received from God?'* However, this is a misunderstanding of that verse, and often used as a clause or excuse for cultural legalism. The verse is in fact speaking about sexual immorality and is nothing at all to do with health. In the same way that many Christians believe you have to dress a certain way, or be educated to a certain level, to speak on behalf of God. They can often be found unconsciously attempting to force middle-class culture upon unsuspecting chavs with regards to health.

Working-class people are often not incredibly bothered about health for many reasons. Often we are found to be working such long hours, with no rights at work, that we don't have time to visit the doctors. With this in mind, it is easy to see why so many working-class people will not seek medical advice until their pain is such that it disrupts their day, or their work.[56] Another reason for the working-class disregard for health is the level of education and language used by those treating them. Mike Sheaff, a senior lecturer at Plymouth University, writes:

> *"Social class has long been noted as a significant factor influencing the quality of patient-*

56 R. Weitz, *The Sociology Of Health, Illness, and Health Care*, (Belmont: Cengage Learning, Inc., 2012), 129-130.

professional interactions, perhaps most obviously in the contrast between private practice and the NHS."[57]

Basically, because we don't use the same language as middle-class people, and so don't understand our doctors, we prefer to go through life in moderate pain. In the same way, we don't care so much about what we eat, we don't care that smoking kills us, and we don't care that alcohol damages our liver. Life is too short to worry about how much shorter it will get if we eat the wrong thing. This means that middle-class people can keep their carrot sticks, and leave the fat on our bacon, hallelujah!!! After all, my bible says that no amount of worrying, carrot sticks, or healthcare can add a minute to my life (Psalm 139:16).

Use What We Have

Lenny 'The Guv'nor' McLean's autobiography was one of the best sellers in the late 90's. As you begin to read it you will notice that this hard-nosed gangster and bare-knuckle fighter constantly refers to a saying. His main aim in life was to 'put steam on the table'. By which he meant his main aim in life was to make sure that his wife

57 M. Sheaff, *Sociology And Health Care*, (Milton Keynes: Open University Press, 2005), 103.

and kids had enough to eat and a roof over their heads.[58] For many working-class people the story is the same. One of the main differences between the classes is the way in which they spend their money. Working-class people tend to spend it as they get it, often living for today or having to scrape by. Middle-class families will often save their money for a rainy day – putting it away in order to increase their material wealth. Whereas upper-class people tend to invest their money, with the aim of making more out of it. Obviously these lines are blurred in some cases, but this along with one or two other differences are the sure-fire way to tell what class you belong to. With this in mind, The Guv'nor, along with many if not all of working-class Britain, will spend all of their money on buying things for their family first, then their close friends, and then on their community. It's just the normal way. It's a lot like what we read about in the book of Acts when the believers in Jerusalem gave everything they had over to their community in order to better serve the greater good. After all, we know that when the money runs out, all we have is each other and so money comes secondary to our family and friends.

---

58 P. Gerrard, *The Guv'nor: A celebration*, (London: Blake Publishing Ltd, 2001), 11-13.

Being a working-class Christian would mean that you don't feel the need to scrimp and save when you have money. You'll be happy to pay your tithe, and give an offering on top, because you know that when it boils down to it: you need your church, friends, and family more than you need your money. The chances are that you may even have the supernatural gift of 'giving' that Schwarz, a Christian writer and practitioner, mentions in his book *The 3 Colors of Ministry*. This gift allows Christians to give material things generously to others. Schwarz claims that this gift does not depend upon prosperity, which means you don't have to be rich in order to give a lot.[59] You have time in abundance, you might have muscles, and you probably have some disposable income that you can use to bless someone. If we are going to be a sub-culture in Christianity that actually does what the bible says we may want to take a leaf out of Gabrielle's book. One day as she was unloading her shopping trolley full of food into her car, she decided that just giving the man selling the Big Issue a pound wasn't enough. She proceeded to walk up to him and offer to buy him his shopping. She brought him a whole bunch of shopping including tins, groceries, milk,

---

59 C. A. Schwarz, *The 3 Colors of Ministry*, (St. Charles: ChurchSmart Resources, 2001), 105.

bread, and even cigarettes.[60] Being a chav Christian will mean going beyond the church's love and grace, and into a world of supernatural love and grace. You can actually be someone's hero today!

Reckless Faith

I was at Reinhard Bonnke's *Fire Conference*, in 2013, when I first heard the phrase 'Reckless Faith'. Everything within me wanted to shout out loud. My personal journey of faith and ministry has been one of reckless faith, and I believe that, if they had a chance, many more of my working-class brothers and sisters would join me. Being poor my whole life – even when I've had money – has led to a place of not caring what people think of me or what I do. At one point I would say that I was almost amoral – in that I deliberately refused to believe in rules or regulations in order to get by from day to day. I was willing to cross any line and walk straight passed any boundary. I sometimes scared myself with how much I didn't care. Society had nothing to offer me, and had never given me anything, which meant that I owed them nothing. Since becoming a Christian I have switched my thinking, but kept my recklessness. In my first few months of being a Christian I rang a football stadium

---

60 P. Scanlon, *The 15 Revolution: Go ahead inconvenience me*, (Bradford: Abundant Life Publishing, 2009), 80-83.

and a rugby stadium in the hope that they would let me fill their stadiums full of worshippers... for free!! My pastor thought I was mad. At one point I went to Wickes and purchased a piece of rope which I proceeded to tie a slipknot in. I approached my pastor and lassoed him whilst telling him "I'm your disciple now!" I am willing to do whatever God tells me, whenever he tells me.

This reckless faith has been instrumental in pioneering our first church, and during my ministry up until this point. I had actually opened a bank account for our new church and put a reasonable amount of cash in the bank, also purchasing a PA kit, before even stepping foot in the town. A lady we ministered to in our first few months was shocked to learn that I believed our first public outreach event was my idea of small – as we fed 400 people at a community barbecue. She had no idea that I had organised the event – which had two bouncy castles and face-paints for up to 650 kids – a year beforehand when I had no volunteers or team members.

We need reckless Christians and we need pastors that are willing to put the effort into teaching faithfulness and maturity to them before letting them loose. We've seen loads of people healed, delivered, and saved during our reckless ministry. You can be the same! The question is 'do you want to be like Peter?' Who got out of the boat and walked on water – recklessly, or do you want to be like one of the passersby? Do you want to be fed, as part of the crowd, or do you want to fly?

Authenticity

If I'm honest, I have one thing that really does make me cringe in the church. I've been around enough Christians and trainee church leaders to experience falsehood. One experience that I had was when we had a guest speaker at bible college who spoke on authenticity. It was in the week leading up to one of our final corporate get togethers. The preacher, a well respected vicar of a local church, spent a good forty minutes explaining to us all the importance of authenticity. During this time he told us that we should dress the same on Sunday morning, whilst preaching, that we do during our time off on Saturday mornings. His words were heralded with amens and many of my colleagues approached him for '*prayer*' and to '*affirm him*'. Within the next day or two the very same students that were amazed at the truth of authenticity were scrambling to get changed between lectures and our special corporate meeting. As authenticity went out of the window, and I was told to take my tracksuit off, I could almost hear the cry of the Holy Spirit: "*this is the future of my church!*"

Authenticity is not just a matter of clothing. It covers lifestyle, integrity, intimacy, spirituality, and emotions. I pray that, through this chapter, you might die to yourself and put an authentic relationship with yourself, God, and those around you above any insecurity that you might otherwise be feeling.

Lifestyle

If authenticity is honesty, then living an authentic lifestyle would mean living an honest lifestyle. By this I don't mean that we are to stop lying and cheating – we should stop doing that because we love Jesus. What I mean is that due to the fact that chavs are less likely to care what people think about us, we should live a life that portrays an honest perception of ourselves. We should be proud of who we are and where we've come from. Not ashamed to use our slang and dress according to how we feel comfortable. You could say that this entire book is all about living an honest, and authentic, lifestyle. Gazza would never have been rated as one of the best footballers in the world if he wasn't flamboyant. There's no doubt that he would have had people, throughout his years growing up, telling him to calm down, or stop being so loud. If UB40 had tried to fit in with the predominant type of music at the time, they would never have had such a huge influence on the music scene. They never would have changed the way that music was used.

If you wear your socks over the bottoms of your trousers, or if you wear a cap in the street, you should wear those things to church on Sundays. If you preach in church, you should be able to preach with your cap on. If you speak with an accent, or use slang, you should do so when speaking at your church. In the early 1900's a Methodist minister thought that the church was too middle-class.[61] This caused him to spend some time searching the mines in Wales for a working-class preacher. His hope was simple – he wanted to encourage working-class people to join the church, and understood that this meant that they needed to understand the preacher. The man he found in the mines was Evan Roberts and, within a very short period of time, the Welsh Revival had kicked off. During the next few years, people from all backgrounds were saved all over Wales. Prisons and pubs were emptied as people committed their lives to Christ. The revival is known as the last massive move of God in our nation, and that was over one hundred years ago. Wouldn't it be good if a movement of

---

61 E. Evans, *The Welsh Revival Of 1904,* (South Wales: Evangelical Press Of Wales, 1969), 49-50.

chav Christians was to bring the next huge move of God?!!

Scripture says to live like Christ, not to live like Maggie Thatcher, or the Jones's. Christ lived the life of a poor man. He had nothing and wanted nothing. His friends and those around him were more important to him than riches, influence, knowledge, or security. You will feel a release as soon as you commit to be you rather than who people want you to be. What's more, God loves you for you, and would prefer an authentic follower – a follower that feels secure in who they are.

Integrity

A lifestyle of authentic integrity means actually living in the holiness that you claim to live. It also means living in the holiness that you tell others to live in. As I've already mentioned, a lot of the rules and regulations that have been put in place for Christians are not Godly at all – they are cultural. Living an integral lifestyle means living the life that you preach. Being the same person on Monday, at work, that you are during the musicians's set on Sunday morning. Let's face it, our nation has been shown the 'old' way of doing church, and spirituality, for the past one hundred years and its success has reached its limit at 2% of our nation being committed Christians. If our post-modern nation is to be reached today we need to live in authentic integrity. This means setting your goals at a reachable level. The bible says that we live under grace, not law, but our legalistic Christian culture leads many middle-class dudes to tell us that holiness equals good manners,; that Godliness equals cleanliness; that maturity equals how long you've been a Christian or your level of education. To be honest it's all rubbish. Jesus would have stank with a lack of soap, or modern hygiene, and he was actually God. The religious people were often dismayed at the people that Jesus hung out with, and the types of things he would come out with – sure he was clever and spoke with authority, but he was so uncultured compared to the religious people of his day. Jesus didn't dress up for any special occasion, he was just his authentic self. He didn't deny his wisdom or power in front of Herod or the Roman rulers. Most important of all, though, is that he didn't blush when the religious people brought a naked women before him to be judged for sleeping with a man that wasn't her husband, and he didn't send away the prostitute that came into the religious ruler's house to anoint him.

In the same way, if we are going to live in authentic integrity we won't feel ashamed of our chav friends. We won't be ashamed to invite our religious friends to our house that might not be decorated in the latest fashion, or smells like we haven't bathed our Staffordshire Bull Terrier for a few months. We won't try to mask who we really are. We'll be honest when we're sitting in a Life Group and are asked "How is your marriage at the moment?" or "Is there anything that you need help with?" No-one is 100% healed, and no-one has it all together. An authentically integral person is able to be honest in front of their peers and has nothing to hide because they are not afraid. I'm a chav and I refuse to fall victim to this world. I am a conquerer!! I shall not be beat down or told what to do. I will live in the grace of an authentically integral lifestyle!

Intimacy

Intimacy is a massive subject that is often overlooked by people. It's overlooked by churches, and it's overlooked by individuals. Our problem starts with our intimacy with ourselves. I was told by my counsellor that intimacy means '*into me see*'[62]. Sometimes we are so afraid of past memories and hurts that we are actually scared to look within ourselves. This fear means that we will not let

---

62 I learnt so much about myself, my emotions, and my relationships from spending time with a qualified counsellor. The fact that Sharon Johnson was Christian made every session feel like a session with the Holy Spirit. There's an old saying that goes '*hurting people hurt people*' and so I've made it my life's mission to be healed in order to heal people.

anyone else look within us, including God. Our fear of intimacy with ourselves means that we cannot be intimate with God. This in turn spreads to our wider circle of friends and family, and we end up living a lonely life despite all of the people that surround us.

I've been unfortunate enough to watch as many people have shaken under the supposed power of the Holy Spirit, only to walk home gossiping about their neighbour's life. I've also been present when someone has lifted their hands to God in worship, as a part of the worship team, and then gone home to sleep with their partner outside of marriage. The simple fact is that if you act the right way in a meeting you can often be given more respect and responsibility in your church. Simply by dressing the right way, and saying the right things, you can be put into a place of leadership over other people's spiritual walks. This is scary! Holiness describes the condition of your heart, not the things that you do in front of the crowds.

During my lifetime on council estates, I have noticed one awesome and Godly trait amongst my peers – people say what they want and mean what they say, even if it offends people. Sure we should be graceful in the way we act, and choose when to say particular things with wisdom. Jesus said that if someone has wronged you, your job is not to embarrass them in front of people, but to go to them privately (Matthew 18:15). As a working-class Christian I would expect that you would be authentic with your intimacy. Let God in, don't be a faker. The fact is that if you need open-heart surgery to be healed, you're going to experience some pain. That pain will bring you life though. None of the uber-Christians that you hear about on the TV, or read about in these epic books, shy away from the Holy Spirit's work within them. It doesn't take three hours of prayer in your cupboard everyday, or fasting two days a week, for you become as powerful as Peter – whose shadow passed by a people and brought the healing presence of God to them (Acts 5:14-16). All you need to do is let God do your open-heart surgery and beg him to possess you with his Holy Spirit. There's not an hour that goes by that I don't feel something of God's presence. Just be open to authentic intimacy with the Holy Spirit, and with yourself. Everything else will follow.

Spirituality

I think that the church's lack of authenticity, with regards to the things that I am looking at in this chapter, can be mostly put down to our insecurity. I can remember times when I've felt as though people are being fake with their spirituality. I often get dismayed at the way that Pentecostals and Charismatics can shout out their tongues during prayer meetings or worship services, but struggle to say hello with a smile to a stranger in the street. I often ask myself, *how come the Holy Spirit doesn't randomly cause people to scream aloud the name of Jesus in Morrison's?* The answer is: our spirituality is not authentic. I look to the those people that sit at the back of church with bible in hand looking for someone that seems distressed or upset, who they can administer their 'pastoral gifting' to, or the old lady that insists she has the gift of discernment and this week you're the one that has demons (probably because you didn't speak in tongues during the service this week). I love the lady at my home church who decides to start praising Jesus when she's giving a lift to a neighbour or a colleague. The lady who then reveals her spirituality with an authenticity that Peter would struggle with (Galatians 2:11-14). This woman is never asked why she's so kind, or why she's so charitable. The answer to these questions is always on show.

At the church that I am pioneering in Lincoln, one of my favourite parts of our vision is that I see people worshipping God authentically. I see people with an open and authentic spirituality: praying in the street for their loved one; wailing and mourning with those that mourn; openly worshipping their saviour in the parks and fields; taking a break at work to pray for their colleagues instead of smoke a cigarette. When Jesus said that we are the light of the world, he said that we shouldn't hide our light (Matthew 5:14-16). This statement begs the question: why do we always hide it behind the church doors? My friends and I, along with many other groups of young people, are constantly frowned upon for loitering near shops and street corners. This is the chav way. We feel comfortable and safe in numbers. Let's be honest it wouldn't take much for a few chav Christians to get together as a group and practice their spirituality openly for all to see outside the shops or on a street corner. I'm excited to say that part of our mission includes lighting a bonfire on my front garden and taking communion with anyone who fancies what I would call '*a manly communion service*'. Young men are attracted to fire like women are attracted the word 'sale'! Let's put our insecurity to one side. Let's be open with our spirituality. Let the world see it. Let them know what an authentic Christian looks like. After all, a chav Christian should be almost aggressive with his/her spirituality, not apologetic or scared what people think about it.

Emotions

I recently woke up in the mood for theology. This is a dangerous thing because I like to think outside the box and my thoughts can often offend religious minds. This one morning in particular I went down to the park for my morning devotions – I simply lay on the floor, or stand in God's presence, at the bandstand. During my time listening to God, he asked me '*why did I say that I would build my church on Peter – The Rock?* I've spent some time meditating on this and I've realised that Peter went through every emotion and situation that could cause him to grow. Take for example the transfiguration. Peter openly (authentically) showed his religious heart and his desire to get things right according the old covenant when he asked if it was time to build new temples (Matthew 17:4). Before Jesus was taken captive by the religious rulers Peter authentically showed that his trust was in his own strength when he said that he would never leave Jesus side, and that he was willing to die with him and for him (Mark 14:29). Peter makes so many mistakes throughout the Gospels and Acts showing that he was authentic with his emotions. Yes he got rebuked, and he failed on occasions, but like a tree we are all made stronger by adjusting ourselves to deal with the winds and rains that come against us. Peter had so many opportunities to grow strong with the storms that came against him that, I believe, Jesus thought he was the safest option with the strongest roots to keep his church standing firm.

Peter went on to make loads more mistakes but at the end of his ministry he died in glory as he was martyred for the sake of his Saviour after taking the gospel to the home of the largest world power of the time – Rome. Being authentic with your emotions means being open with them so that God can use them to teach you. How are you supposed to be healed of a damaged emotion if you keep it secret.

Peter is a great example of living an authentic lifestyle, let's face it: his emotional intelligence levels would have been through the roof after all the stuff that he had to learn the hard way. He showed authentic faith when he stepped out of the boat (Matthew 14:28-29), and showed authentic spirituality when he walked out in front of three thousand people and preached Jesus on the day of Pentecost (Acts 2:14-41). Peter had no inhibitions as he served Jesus, like a chav, all the way to Rome. You have this same opportunity.

Worship

Worship is a huge part of our spirituality as believers and followers of Jesus. As an open and authentic working-class Christian I spend more time in worship than I do reading my bible or any other spiritual act. During the last few years I have been really intrigued to find out why we worship the way we do, and to find out whether we worship this way because it is expected or because it is authentic. To my surprise I have found out that the Pentecostal form of worship has actually been born out of a working-class spirituality – which may explain why it looks so awkward when middle-class church tries to loose themselves in worship. This chapter will explore the psychology and history behind authentic working-class worship.

The Psychology Behind It

Harvard sociology lecturer, Timothy Nelson claims that there is a link between your social standing and your preferred style of worship and, although his research has taken place primarily in American culture, I can see a lot of truth in his assertions with regard to working-class culture in Britain. Nelson also makes a connection between the working-class mechanism of expressing themselves – that of excessive alcohol consumption, promiscuous sex, banter, and rowdy behaviour – and their struggles, to explain their style of worship. Nelson tells his readers that explosive or dramatic worship and dancing brings a psychological release from day to day struggles and worries.[63] However, Nelson also explains that these perceptions of working-class expression come from a middle-class bias. Coming from a working-class background, I would prefer to say that negative traits such as excessive alcohol consumption and promiscuous sex are not confined to the lower classes, but are merely more freely discussed due to a different social etiquette. These negative traits are equally common in all classes,[64] but social expectations prevent openness regarding these issues amongst other classes.

It is also my own experience that working-class people need to express themselves, often in a 'larger than life' manner. From an insider's perspective I can say that on

---

63 Timothy J. Nelson, "At ease with our own kind: Worship practices and class segregation in American religion," in *Religion and Class in America: culture, history and politics*, eds. S. McCloud & W. A. Mirola, (Leiden: Brill, 2008), 50.

64 R. Smith & R. Womack, The Telegraph, '*Middle class are biggest abusers of alcohol*', http://www.telegraph.co.uk/news/uknews/1566292/Middle-class-are-biggest-abusers-of-alcohol.html, accessed 17th May 2013.

many occasions I have used alcohol, drugs, and anti-social behaviour to hit back at the society that has tried to control me. Let me make it clear now though, I am now a new creation – as are you. I still feel that I need to express myself, but I need to do so with the heart of Jesus. This chapter will move on to explore the experiences of those that have gone before us, and seek to show the ways in which we can feel fulfilled and relieved by our flamboyant expressions of worship and love.

Early Days Of The Pentecostal Movement

Many writers consider the Welsh Revival to be the catalyst that started the Pentecostal Movement in Britain.[65] At the turn of the Twentieth Century Seth Joshua, one of the first ministers of the Welsh Revival[66], felt that there was a danger of the church being overtaken by ministers with academic gifts rather than spiritual gifts, and so he began to pray. Eventually he felt

---

65 W. K. Kay, *Pentecostals in Britain*, (Cumbria: Paternoster Press, 2000), 1; *K. Warrington, Pentecostal Theology: A theology of encounter,* (London: T & T Clark, 2008), 4; A writer from the Barnsley Chronicle writing about one of Jeffreys meetings likened them to the Welsh Revival claiming that the same spirit of reverence that swept through Jeffreys' meetings was the same as that of the Welsh Revival; W. G. Hathaway (ed.), "*Marvels of Healing*," The Elim Evangel, Vol xii Nos. 51 & 52 (1931), 28-29.

66 E. Evans, *The Welsh Revival of 1904*, 49-50.

that God was telling him to take someone with a working-class background to learn to preach. He soon stumbled across Evan Roberts in the mines and put him to use in the church as a minister in training. Within months the Welsh Revival had kicked-off through the ministry of Roberts.[67] The revival quickly spread across Wales and it was noted that the most dramatic results of the revival were coming from the non-conformist churches rather than the Anglican ones. William Kay, a well-known Pentecostal writer, says there was *'evidence that the Anglican community benefited from what was happening among its less socially exalted neighbours.'*[68]

One of the products to come out of the Welsh Revival was the founder of the Elim Pentecostal Movement, George Jeffreys. His ideas of ministry to the working-class may have stemmed from his connections with the Salvation Army with which he was constantly linked.[69] Smith Wigglesworth was another well-known evangelist from a working-class background, he had also been linked with the Salvation Army, but left the denomination when they refused to let him marry the woman that

---

67 *ibid*, 63.
68 Kay, *Pentecostals in Britain*, 8-9.
69 M. R. Hathaway, 'The Elim Pentecostal Church: Origins, development, and distinctives', K. Warrington (eds.) *Pentecostal Perspectives*, (Carlisle: Paternoster Press, 1998), 19.

would later become his wife due to their legalistic rules about relationships within the corps.[70] It seems that Elim was not a middle-class territorial church, but was in fact a movement that Jeffreys and his evangelistic workers kept progressing. According to one writer '*members were drawn primarily from the poor working class, factory workers and labourers, who had previously been non-conformists*'.[71] In particular it was a movement that had an urgency to see people come to faith from lives of addiction and poverty. Elim was founded by the working-class, and driven by their work ethic and their deep conviction that salvation mattered more than living a stately life or moving up the social ladder. Another writer goes as far as to write:

> "*At least in the congregations I studied, the upper class, the upper middle, and what, for want of a better term, I will call the established middle classes (persons whose education, occupation, and income assure them of a reasonably secure and comfortable, though not especially affluent standard of living) were not in evidence in these churches or in any of the Pentecostal churches I visited.*"[72]

---

70 Wilson, *Wigglesworth*, 20-23.

71 N. Toulis, *Believing Identity: Pentecostalism and the meditation of Jamaican ethnicity and gender in England*, (Oxford: Berg, 1997), 117.

72 G. Schwartz, *Sect Ideologies and Social Status*, (Chicago: The

Churches would not try to change the activities, or occupations, of the congregation, but would instead send them out of their meetings with a desire to express their faith in everyday life.[73] You could say that Elim was not concerned with changing the culture or class of its members, but was more interested in seeing more people come to the knowledge of Jesus as Saviour.

It is fair to say that the Pentecostal Movement was a thoroughly working-class affair. So, when we look at their style of worship with regard to what Timothy Nelson wrote, we will not be surprised. In the early days of the working-class Pentecostal Movement the participation of every member was valued instead of the preaching of an ordained minister. This meant that every meeting was unpredictable, giving a sense of excitement to the people that attended. Apparently they never knew what to expect next because no-one knew what the Spirit would prompt from one minute to the next.[74] The press using words, or phrases, like '*improvisation*' and '*organised chaos*' was the norm of the day.

University of Chicago Press, 1970), 192.

73 B. R. Wilson, *Sects and Society: the sociology of three religious groups in Britain*, (London: William Heinemann LTD, 1961), 78.

74 W. Kay, *Pentecostalism: A very short introduction*, (Oxford: Oxford University Press, 2011), 83-84.

With all of the articles that I've read from the old Elim Evangel and Confidence magazines, I can almost imagine a scene of what most of us would call chaos as people would shout out randomly, sometimes in English and sometimes in tongues. I could imagine that sometimes it would be difficult to get a sermon in whilst people were bringing their own spirituality and worship as the Spirit led. I can also understand why middle-class people found it frustrating because they need structure in order to feel secure. This is why they only allow the Spirit into their services for five minutes after the music has stopped. There are lessons that we can learn if we take a look at the past whilst researching the psychology and thinking of working-class people, which will help us to worship more effectively as working-class Christians.

What It Means For Us

The Pentecostal Movement saw more people find faith than any other movement in British history. George Jeffreys is still regarded as Britain's most fruitful evangelist, and Smith Wigglesworth is still spoken about and studied, despite his controversial methods, to this day. My question is: *can a working-class liturgy, minister, and style of music bring about the same sort of revival once again? And if it can, what does a working-class worship service look like today?*

In this section I would like to look at some areas of interest among the original Pentecostals with the aim of encouraging the same sort of behaviour and openness. These areas of intrigue include popular music, attractive speakers, spiritual freedom, and larger than life stories and testimonies.

- **Popular music**: Since the beginning of the Pentecostal movement the Spirit-filled services were known for their very modern music, often using popular tunes, like the Salvation Army's jaunty music-hall style of worship or Caribbean styles of music.[75] I was excited to find that the Pentecostal church where I became a Christian used drums and guitars during their music sets, and I was shocked when one day the lead musician played a little bit of Michael Jackson and Busted during his worship set. I thought it was brilliant. It helped me to know that the church was a place that my friends and family might find fun too. In our church, in Lincoln, we make a point of listening to chart music with the aim of finding songs that can be used to worship

75 Wilson, *Wigglesworth*, 19; Warrington, *Pentecostal Theology*, 224-225; A. Anderson, *An Introduction To Pentecostalism: Global Charismatic Christianity*, (Cambridge,:Cambridge University Press, 2004), 65-66.

God. My take on it is that God doesn't just redeem me and my attitudes, he also redeems the world and the things in the world. For example, the music. One song in particular that we have been playing recently is written by chart-topping singer and song-writer, Emeli Sande. Part of her song, *River*, goes like this:

"If all you want are answers to your questions
And you can't seem to find no love for free
If you're looking for the right direction
Then darling, look for me
See, I can make the load much lighter
I just need you to confide in me
But if you're to proud to follow rivers
How you ever gunna find the sea?'

Church should be as attractive as possible. Paul said to win as many people as you can by any means possible (1 Corinthians 9:22), and we can see popular music's impact on the revivals of the past. There are three things that attract large crowds in our culture: music, sports, and attractive speakers or comedians.

- **Attractive speakers**: One of my favourite historical writers, Donald Gee, writing about Smith Wigglesworth claimed that by 1925 there were not many places left on earth that hadn't been touched by the evangelist. Whether Gee was travelling across Arizona or visiting New Zealand, it seemed that he couldn't get away from people speaking about Smith Wigglesworth. Donald Gee even goes on to say that some of the smaller, more private, churches felt quite embarrassed about the limelight that came their way through the ministry of some of these old Pentecostal heroes.[76] Writing about George Jeffreys Gee says:

"In addition to the all-important enduement of power from on high, he proved to have outstanding ability as an evangelist, and expositor of the Word of God. Coupled with this he was gifted with a voice of a great musical beauty as a preacher, a striking appearance, and that subtle quality known as "personality." Obviously he was a born leader."[77]

Personally I've always wondered why Christians feel so offended at the prospect of a Christian-celebrity. I've come to the conclusion that it must be either false-humility or a misunderstanding of humility. Being humble isn't putting yourself

76 Gee, *The Pentecostal Movement*, 149-150.
77 *Ibid*, 106-107.

down, or trying to be less than you are. It is merely accepting who you are. Jesus knew that he was God and lived in that knowledge, at no point did he ever tell people not to worship him. In fact, he encouraged people to worship him (Luke 19:35-40). This isn't to say that we should worship Christian-celebrities rather we should be aware that there is nothing wrong with being respected or being put on a pedestal. Actually, if you look at our culture, post-modern culture trusts nothing and no-one, that is except for big brands and big celebrities. You know what you're getting from a Mars Bar, and the importance of celebrities is shown between every program we watch on the TV. Charities rely on celebrities to build trust, companies use celebrities to build trust, and brands use celebrities to build trust. The one thing that the church is missing at the moment is trust! It doesn't take a rocket-scientist to work this one out.

- **Larger than life stories**: The stories about these great men of God spread all over our land, as media outlets told the world what was going on in their meetings. I've read stories about new limbs growing back, and hideous growths falling away from people's bodies.[78] Working-class culture loves the drama of a larger than life story, and although some of the stories were exaggerated, many of them were 100% true. The church may have been guilty of giving a rather tame picture of God and his awesome power over the years of conservative evangelicalism. I've found, however, that my working-class colleagues are very excited to hear of the awesome things that I have experienced in my spiritual walk. If God has given you a taste of the glory of heaven, you'd have to be extremely misguided or spiteful not to share it with the rest of the world. My advice to working-class Christians, and people that want to minister to working-class people, is tell your story and tell it proudly. If someone else exaggerates it the next time they tell their friend, you can always correct them. The only person being glorified is Jesus, and we should be glorifying him as much as possible.

- **Spiritual freedom**: In Genesis 1 we can see that the Holy Spirit brings order to the chaos of the waters as he hovers over them. There is freedom in order. In the same way that a football referee

---

78 Wilson, *Wigglesworth*, 184.

brings order to the game to make it playable and safe, so we need people to lead a service with order as well as freedom. However, we should never be held captive by our liturgy. If God is drawing the service away from a preach and into an hour of worship, we should be able to do as the Spirit says. It seems that thanks to Luther, and sola scriptura[79], the church has made the preach the most important thing in a service. We seem to put teaching, and then worship, above what the Holy Spirit is doing. A service for working-class people would be more scriptural than scripture. Let's get together and see what the Holy Spirit does, whilst keeping order through anointed leadership. A supernatural leader can stay organised and ordered during what can look like the chaos of the Holy Spirit moving, and likewise working-class believers should be open to the Holy Spirit during times of teaching. Donald Gee writes:

"*Once the Spirit of God is recognised as operating quite as truly in teaching as in prophesying, and as revealing Himself quite as surely in the Holy Scriptures as in His outward manifestations, then believers are well*

---

79 The belief that God only speaks through scripture.

on the royal road to a sane enjoyment of the rich fullness of a continual experience of Pentecostal power and blessing."[80]

Ultimately our experience of the Holy Spirit shouldn't be confined to the limit of other people's experiences, and what works for middle-class culture doesn't always work for chav culture. A lot of the traditions that middle-class Pentecostal and Charismatic churches practice come out of a working-class experience of spirituality. It seems that the experience that we see practiced weekly falls way short of that first experience that shook the British Isles at the turn of the last century. Maybe by exploring the past we can better understand how to change the future of our nation.

---

80 Gee, *The Pentecostal Movement*, 81.

Teaching & Preaching

There have been countless times when I've sat through a talk at church and not understood a word the preacher is saying. There have also been many many times when my working-class friends have told me that there is a disconnect between their lives and the lives of the people that are preaching to them. I've heard single mums asking why there's no teaching on raising their kids, or why there's no teaching on how to win their estranged boyfriends for Jesus. Young men asking why all the preachers are ever so keen to teach them about tithing, but not so keen to teach them how to get a job. I've come to notice that most pastors are so busy that when you get five minutes with them, they just want to talk business. Sometimes I feel like just sitting with some of my colleagues and asking them if they will be my friend. I'm not interested in business, business tires me. I need a friend that I can do life with, who struggles and then gets over it. I need to learn from their struggles and experience. Needless to say, there are many ways in which we learn, and in which we need to teach.

Education

According to Owen Jones, a social and political writer with the Guardian, a fifth of all boys that are eligible for free school dinners don't obtain five GCSEs.[81] This may be due to the lack of equality with regards to the opportunities that are offered in education. It is widely accepted that even for students of the same ability, there is a gaping difference in educational achievement between the classes.[82] Some believe that this may be due to cultural deprivation and the fact that working-class pupils find it difficult to understand the values, attitudes, and language of the the predominantly white middle-class culture of the education system.[83] Basically, working-class people struggle in education because the system is setup specifically so that middle-class children do better. The words used in schools, colleges, and universities are middle-class and so middle-class children find it easier to succeed. However, the rest of us struggle.

What this means for the church is that we need to tailor our language to the culture in which we seek to minister. I had the privilege of spending three years at university, studying Theology, during which time I learnt about lots

---

81 Jones, *Chavs*, 172.

82 K. Browne, *Introducing Sociology For AS Level*, (Oxford: Polity Press, 2006), 251.

83 *Ibid*, 257.

of 'ologies'. Words that explain what you are studying. For example, theology is the study of God, and pneumatology is the study of the Holy Spirit. However, even during my time there, people would say words to me that I knew nothing about. I would often have to go away to check out what a word meant after spending time with a largely middle-class crowd. What's more, when I finished college and started speaking to 'normal' people, they would often have to ask me what words meant. Now put this information into a working-class environment, where people are notoriously cynical about education – mainly because we're made to sit through fourteen years of schooling just to work in McDonald's – and suddenly the church feels a million miles away from reality, not just because of the way they dress, or their ambitions and heavenly mindedness, but the very way in which we use language. My advice to the church is learn some slang, and my advice to my fellow chavs is read a few small books. Your best bet is to read small books that are easy to read and informational to begin with because you'll be able to celebrate an easy win when you finish, and you would have learnt something in the meantime. This will bring the world of reading and learning to life for you. It will mean that when you apply for a job you will be more likely to want to understand, or even be able to understand already, what your future employer wants from you and what he's saying. To let you know, I don't intend to patronise you with this advice. I never read a book before I became a Christian. By following this advice myself, I won a peer award at the end of my first year of bible college. The award was the Sally Gibbs award. She was our librarian, and the award was for the most well read student – the student that everyone believed had read the most. That summer I went on to read fourteen books during the break between my first and second years. That's redemption!!

Experiential Teaching

There is one way in which working-class people have been learning effectively for decades. Apprenticeships give people the opportunity to learn on the job whilst earning a small amount of cash. Discipleship is all about doing life together. Faith comes through hearing, but the ability to listen comes through experience.

In my spiritual walk I have found that my most precious lessons in life have come through supernatural experiences. My faith is strong because I don't believe in God, I know him! Recently I've been meditating on intimacy and what it means for Christians, and I've come to the conclusion that Christians have a really bad habit of walking into a place that is drenched in God's presence only to begin praying for everyone else except themselves. It's the greatest tragedy to hit our faith. We can walk into the place where God holds healing and deliverance for us, and miss it because we religiously start to look to the world and our families or friends as a way to get out of the awkwardness of handing God the keys to our innermost hurts and emotions. What's more, we squander the opportunity to experience the supernatural, and learn from the Holy Spirit, something that could never be taught by the brightest theologians.

An example of one of my own supernatural experiences, that strengthened my faith as a young Christian, was when in a prayer meeting I prayed "*Lord, if Moses could see your glory when he wasn't washed in your blood, when he was covered in sin, then I should be allowed to as well. I want to see your glory!*" Almost immediately God made me feel extremely tired which was very unusual for me because I'm an activist. I fought for about five minutes against the urge to let go and fall asleep. Eventually I felt as though God may be bringing it on and that I should have grace with myself – after all, the other lads in the prayer meeting fell asleep every week. As soon as I let go, God gave me a really vivid dream where I found myself in front of an extremely bright cloud. If you ever saw magnesium burn in a science lesson, then you'll get an idea of how bright the cloud was. I was in awe. I thought that this was God's glory, but he said "*Come inside!*" Feeling a boldness to do so, I began to walk into the cloud where a giant figure of a man stood, dressed all in black with gold laces, like ribbons, tied around his arms and legs. As I knelt before him he said "*Look at my face!*" Scared out of my pants I began to raise my head. I had made the decision, at that point, that I was willing to die to see God's glory. However, as my eyes reached his shins fear kicked in and I collapsed in a flood of tears with shear amazement at how awesome God really is. You could also experience the same sort of awesome things if you just put your full trust in God. In order to totally trust in God you will need to trust him with your life and your emotions as you come into his presence. Start your Holy Spirit apprenticeship today, don't wait, find somewhere to pray.

Preaching

I've been asking the question for a couple of years now: How do we preach effectively to working-class people? As I've already mentioned, lots of quotes that might include some really clever analogies or theological words might not work amongst working-class people. If I had a pound for every time I heard an analogy or clever sounding joke during a preach that I didn't understand, I would have a lot more money to spend on evangelism. However, if we look at working-class culture we might be able to pull some things out that might help us in our preaching. Let me first explain that preaching and teaching are two totally different animals. I believe teaching is for equipping and challenging individuals in their walk with God and the doctrines, or core beliefs, that structure their life. Preaching, however, is used for motivating, inspiring, and calling for a response in a person's life to bring them closer to God. Sometimes it might even be used for correcting or rebuking – only if the preacher has the right motives, I might add.

So, what things can we pull out of working-class culture to help us figure out the best way to preach. The first thing I'd mention is the banter. We all like a good laugh, and it helps to build relationship. If we are asking people to change their life trajectory or make a response to something that God is doing, then it needs to come through relationship. In working-class culture there's nothing better than beer or banter to build stronger relationships, and I'm not sure what people would think about cracking open a few Stellas before a service. So let's stick with banter. Hallelujah! Lots of people, both working-class and middle-class, are happy to sit through two hours of a comedian telling jokes, but they might not be willing to sit through thirty minutes of stodgy dogmatic rambling from a preacher. I like to think that God gave us a sense humour for a reason, and that the bible doesn't tell us to repent from it when we get saved.

The second thing that is important when preaching to any crowd, but in particular a working-class crowd, is storytelling. We already discussed how the ability to tell stories in our culture is important, as it's one of the best ways to get the local news. Whether you're a builder in a pub, or a mum at the school gate, you will find that there are storytellers all around you. We love storytelling. What's more, these stories are the things of faith. They cause us to get excited and it's at these times that we begin to open our worldview up for criticism.

One example of a great preacher and teacher that uses both of these with expertise is Jeff Lucas. This dude can have his audience in stitches. Once people are laughing and joking with him they drop their guard, allowing him to minister into their hearts and lives with precision. It's at these times that he tells some of his most moving stories, causing a heart reaction that can be hard to find in some of our churches. Let's face it, the bible says that God's word should never come back void, which means that if we are truly speaking the word of God there should be some sort of response. By tailoring our preaching to our audience we can help people make the jump from life to death with very little in the way. By using a couple of simple tools we can remove roadblocks between our congregations and their futures.

Warning: Things to watch out for

Whilst beginning to write this book, I felt that my main aim was to highlight areas in working-class culture that could bring something positive to the church. Although there are many good things in working-class culture that could help the church and bring us closer to Jesus – some of which I still haven't mentioned due to space – there are some things amongst the classes that aren't cultural at all, simply put... they are sin! During this chapter I am not interested in pointing out the faults of the middle-class, I am purely thinking of helping my own people – the working-class. Unfortunately during this chapter it may feel like I directly target some people. Let me tell you that the chances are that I don't know you. If your heart begins to beat faster, you feel afraid, and a presence within is urging you to change your life, that is the Holy Spirit, not condemnation. Hallelujah!

I'm just going to mention a few things, and I'm not looking to go into too much detail. There will be no testimonies of where other people have sinned, but I may mention some of my own sin. I pray right now that your world, and my world, will be changed as we head into this subject. Amen!

Gossip

There is a difference between gossip and storytelling. The main difference is that when you gossip you are telling the story of someone else. A lot of the time the story is demeaning, and can often be hurtful. The way to know whether you are gossiping or not is to ask yourself: would I say this in front the person that I am talking about? If the answer is no, then you shouldn't be saying it at all because it's sin! Christians are not in competition with each other, the secular world is. In heaven you don't trample the people around you in order to be lifted up, you put yourself underneath your peers to lift them up.

> *"In your relationships with each other, have the same mindset as Christ. Who, being in very nature God, did not consider equality with God something to be used to his advantage; rather making himself nothing by taking the very nature of a servant, being made in human likeness. And being found in appearance as a man, he humbled himself by becoming obedient to death – even death on a cross!*

Therefore, God exalted him to the highest place and gave him the name that is above every name."

Philippians 2:5-9

Jesus died so that you could be resurrected. You may need to put your own ambitions to one side in order for God to be glorified.

Sex

God's heart and his plan has always been to protect his sons and daughters. He doesn't want you to do harm to yourself, or to other people. As I've gone through my journey with Christ, one thing seems to crop up again and again. There are so many people that have been hurt because they have had sex outside of a right relationship. A relationship is a mutual love for one another that is confirmed by what you give, not what you take. Relationships are like a beautiful cake. You need a decent foundation on the base layer in order for it to stand strong. Then you need to add your strengths together to build something that tastes amazing – for example, one person might bring some great mothering skills to the relationship. This is like the strawberry jam. Whilst the other might bring the ability to budget. This is like the cream. Together they are amazing and make a beautiful cake. Once the cake is iced with a beautiful white robe – the wedding garments, you put the cherry on the top. This is sex. My challenge to you is: if you want a healthy lifestyle for your children and their children, and their children after that, don't let someone take your cherry without building the right foundations.

Our children are not our meal ticket

Don't get me wrong, I'm not reinforcing the negative stereotype that this is a widespread problem that is inherent of working-class culture. However, this is an issue I feel I need to address. I personally knew that if I had a child, the council would give me a flat. It's something that we're all told as we grow up on a council estate. What's more, we're told that we can get benefits and a nice little £500 grant to get a buggy with too. As times have gone by people have begun to claim that their children have learning disabilities to get more benefits too, and I have increasingly seen parents that are desperate to get their child diagnosed with some sort of behavioural disorder in order to reap the benefits. Now this isn't the case with all parents, so if your child struggles behaviourally or mentally and is on medication then please, shrug this off. The government give extra benefits to people that have children with these problems and I've watched as lots of parents seek a higher income by getting their children diagnosed. I want to say this loud and clear: **Your child is not your meal ticket!** Neither are they your cigarette ticket, or your beer ticket, or your housing benefit ticket. Your child is a person that God loves. They are innocent and free, and don't need the burdens that you place on them. You will have to account for this behaviour when you reach your maker in heaven. You have been blessed with freedom by the grace of God at the cross, and God fully expects you to bless your children with the same freedom. You should be telling them how awesome they are, and how clever they are; not how messed up they are or enslaved they are by their behaviour. Hallelujah!!

Remember your manners

Although this book is all about representing your culture with pride, and redeeming it to make it godly, it's important for us to remember that we are witnesses for Jesus first. This means that when there are people that don't understand our culture or our language, we should make the effort to meet them at their level. What's more, our job as Christians is not just to be a good witness to not-yet-Christians, we should also be a good witness to other Christians. It wasn't long ago that I was telling a church about my vision to pioneer a Chav Church and a more mature lady came up to me after the service to ask what a chav is. The sheer amount of middle-class people that still feel that the word chav is derogatory – not realising that by claiming it as derogatory they are the ones that are giving it this meaning – is incredible. Let's face it, if people stopped using the word in a derogatory manner it wouldn't be derogatory anymore. So when people come to you and complain that you are using a derogatory term, just gently inform them that it is their own oppression that has made it derogatory. My point here though is that you need to remember that you are a Christian first, and chav second. A smile can win a thousand souls. Amen!

Addictive behaviours

There are so many addictive behaviours that a mere paragraph in a chapter is not enough to go too far into detail. With this in mind, I'll just let you know some of them, and pray that if any of them hit a Holy Spirit nerve in you, that you'll find some books or a counsellor to help you out. Addictive patterns that are common in culture could include: approval addiction; addiction to cigarettes or alcohol; addiction to being the centre of attention; addiction to illness; addiction to drugs, both legal and illegal; addiction to work; addiction to sex, or the affirmation that you think you get from it; and addiction to buying things that you can't afford.

I was at an Elim conference a few years back and heard a lady called Sally Livingstone speaking about addictive behaviours in people that commit to following Jesus. As I listened I put myself under the telescope and decided that I would consult a counsellor. My life hasn't been the same since. The thing that had such a huge impact on my life was how Sally explained that when people with addictive backgrounds get saved, they can often become addicted to serving in the church. They receive a handsome reward in the praise of others and the feel-good factor that serving a good cause can bring. I realised that I could well be addicted to serving, and the only way to find out for sure was to take six weeks out of serving in church. The question was: could I cope with just sitting on my bum? And could I turn down opportunities to speak or preach – to be in the spotlight? Gladly, the answer was "yes", I can cope with not serving or being in the spotlight. My question is this: can you?

Violence

It's quite easy for me to talk about most of the things in this chapter because I have experienced, or partaken in, a lot of them. My violent attitude towards people was due to the abuse, and neglect, that I suffered as a child. In my life I had decided that no-one would hurt me if I hurt them first. This meant that if anything went contrary to how I wanted it to go, I would put on my angry mask and become aggressive towards people. Once again, this didn't really stop until I began to speak to my counsellor. Sure, I stopped punching people in the face when I became a follower of Jesus, but I still had a violent demeanour at times. As I sat with my counsellor, I learnt about my emotions and why I act the way I do. My anger was acting as a mask to hide my real emotions which were quite often fear, vulnerability, or insecurity. My anger and violence weren't a part of my upbringing or culture, they were a part of my pain. Although I have a right to feel pain, I don't have the right to inflict it. I'm called to love, and so are you.

Stop being a victim – Hypochondriacs

The subtitle above this paragraph might sound a little harsh or forthcoming, but the fact is that this is something that needs to be said, and this may be the best way for you to hear it. You can see from reading this book that I genuinely care about you and the people that surround you, and there's only one person that knows that this is for you – and that's you! Your pastor probably couldn't tell you this, and neither could your friends, but you're trapped in a cycle of addiction that is damaging your relationships and your self-confidence. To tell a story now would be inappropriate so I'll just stick with what you need to know. You are not a victim. God has made you more than a conqueror. You have been set free. I pray right now that as you are reading this you will think of someone in your church that is trustworthy and faithful enough for you to ask to hold you accountable. I pray that your close friends or spouse will be able to give you the affirmation and attention that you desire, and need! I pray that you will receive a desire to shake free from this addiction in the name of Jesus. Hallelujah!

Denial is as bad as lying

We need to take responsibility for our actions, no matter how shameful they are or how much damage they have done. It pains me to watch as people live a life where they lie to themselves, and those around them in spite of their pain. The truth is that if we could just admit when we've been wrong, and accept our responsibility in hurting others and ourselves, we will be set free. The bible says that the truth will set us free, and this means in many respects.

When we talk about the things that we feel ashamed about, we bring it them into the light of God, and as we do so we relinquish the hold that the enemy of God has on them. I was meditating on this exact subject when I felt as though God asked me how I would feel if I stood in front of him naked – like Adam. Would I cower and try to cover myself in shame? Or would I acknowledge that by stepping into his light I am able to remove my shame and receive forgiveness. The fact is that God was never calling out Adam to laugh at him or to embarrass him. I believe that God was calling him out to cover him with his arms and clothe him in the glory and grace that he had recently given up. In the same way, you can receive forgiveness, grace, and glory by coming out from behind the thorns and thistles to embrace your Father, God! What's more, you can bring healing to those loved ones that you once hurt.

What's Next

Before we come to the end of this book, we need to realise that there is still more for us to learn, there is more for us to experience, and there is more for us to receive from God. Here are just a few tips that should catapult you into a fulfilling spiritual and intellectual journey as you walk with God. It's at this point that I would explain that the experiences mentioned in this book have been watered-down. God has done some amazing supernatural things in my own spiritual walk, and in the journey of those around me. My message to you is that there is always more. There is an experience waiting for you that will blow your mind, and when you receive it, I want you to be in the place to run with it and change this world for Jesus. So let's draw this to a close.

Get stuck into a church and represent

As I've already mentioned, sometimes we need to be a good witness to our Christian brothers and sisters as well as to those that don't already know God. This means showing the local church what a working-class spirituality looks like. Now imagine some people from the local estate walking into a church to see that there is no working-class representative present. This is the case in so many churches that it is unreal. We get stared at and sometimes we even get whispered about. We can feel like we're not welcome, or that our children are not welcome. Ultimately, this is not a reason to forget about God, or to leave the church, but it is difficult to feel alone in a place where you're already vulnerable and our job is to take as many of the roadblocks away from between God and people. You could make the difference between a family entering heaven or not. What's more, if you serve wholeheartedly and lift up your pastor and his vision for the future above your own, there's a good chance that he will begin to give you roles in leadership. You will begin to shape the culture of your church and may be able to bring a more relevant experience of church to your neighbourhood. You could actually change your church and see your city, or town, saved for Jesus. But first you need to get behind your pastor and show that you love him, and that you love Jesus despite how you might talk or dress.

There are lots of websites that can help you find a good church if you don't already belong to one. My hope is that if you have read this book as someone who doesn't already follow Jesus, that you might have seen something within these pages that gives you reason to believe.

Hopefully as you take a step of faith and join a church, beginning to chase after God, he will show you so much more than what's mentioned here. Eventually you will be like me and be able to say "I don't believe in God, I know that he is with me – I don't think he's here, I know he's here!"

Get reading – some books to read

I always get really excited and feel affirmed as I near the end of a book, especially if it's a good one. With this in mind I will not write much in this section. I merely want to give you some ideas of good books to read to follow on from this one. At the end of the day, this book doesn't go very deep at all, and I would like to pass on some of my own favourite books, some of which are life changing, so that you can grow spiritually.

Servolution – by Dino Rizzo: All of these books have inspired me and challenged me to live differently, but no other as much as Servolution. I would constantly be looking at Dino Rizzo's experiences and wondering why the Christians around me were not doing the same. This book will rock your idea of ministry.

Wigglesworth: The complete story – by Julian Wilson: The story of Smith Wigglesworth's journey to receiving the baptism in the Holy Spirit had me on my knees every night for a week whilst I was on mission in

Scarborough. Towards the end of the week I barely thought that I was saved, and I ended up making a new prayer that I still pray on a regular basis today: "Lord, save me again. I'm desperate for your presence and your life!" Wigglesworth's desire for holiness is the biggest inspiration to my life as of yet.

The Five Love Languages – by Gary Chapman: Gary Chapman is an American author who has taken the time to study the ways in which we receive, and give, love. In his book his explains that we all have a 'love-tank', and that there are different ways in which our love-tank is filled up. For some of us it is touch, and for others it is quality time. This book has changed my marriage, my ministry, and my fathering forever. It's an excellent read.

Sacred Pathways – by Gary Thomas: In the same way that Gary Chapman tells us about our love languages, Gary Thomas explains how we all have different ways of reaching God. When I first started bible college, I actually believed that I was the only person that was saved on campus. There didn't seem to be another person that wholeheartedly acted on their faith for miles around. Everyone just wanted to study. By the time I had read my way through loads of books over the summer, including this one in particular, I realised that the people around me were saved and that they merely had different ways of connecting with God.

Courageous Leadership – by Bill Hybels: This was another one of those books that I read during the period between my first and second years of college. Bill Hybels is an amazing leader who is very honest about his spiritual walk. From reading this book you can learn what it means to be a real leader in God's kingdom, and what it means to further his kingdom instead of your own. In reading this book I learnt that character comes before gifting, and that rest is important for the man that wants his ministry to last a lifetime.

The Pentecostal Movement – by Donald Gee: I love reading some of the old stories of the blokes that started the Pentecostal movement. I love to read about how this originally working-class movement came about, and how it worked. What made it tick, and what can bring about the same move of God today. This book has now been made available again on Amazon for people like you and me to buy. Often we can learn the most about the future by looking at the past, and if for nothing else, you should read this book for it's awesome testimony.

Slugs, Snails, and Puppy Dog Tails – by Carolyn Edwards: By reading this book, I learnt how to minister, and be a good father, to my son. We should spend more time learning about our children and how to look after them. Like adults, they also have love tanks, and when we get to heaven God won't ask how many people we led into his presence, or how big our churches are. He'll be asking what happened to the spirituality of the closest people to us – our wives and our children.

Loving God Up Close – by Calvin Miller: Calvin Miller almost puts my scientific, logical mind and the Spirit into one arena and then makes sense of all my previous experience as a prayer warrior and Pentecostal minister. I purchased this book after God gave me this amazing desire to draw closer to his Holy Spirit, knowing the whole time that it meant that I would draw closer to him. You can too, whilst also engaging your brain. This is a great book for a theologian that wants a deeper experience of the Spirit.

As well as all of these books, I would recommend that you check out some of the books in my bibliography if you are interested in working-class culture and spirituality. There is so much more to learn about this subject, and I can only hope that I inspire some other people to take my research and experience a step further.

Get off your backside and tell your friends about Jesus

If we are going to change the world, and the church, we need to be doing it in our droves. For this to happen you will need to tell your chav mates that Jesus is relevant to them too. You will need to let them know that they don't need to become middle-class in order to get into heaven. And you need to tell them that there is an uprising about to happen where God comes back to their neighbourhood, and their schools, and their workplace. Tell your story, share your faith, and share your hope.

Pray for power and holiness

Last but not least, pray for the Spirit of power and holiness to make you the very best witness that you can be. Without the Holy Spirit you are acting out of the flesh, which is weak and feeble. You cannot change the world without the Spirit of God guiding and empowering you to do so. In fact, you won't be able to keep up the stamina or desire to change the world without the Spirit of God. Pray for the fire of God to change you so that you can change the world. Amen! I will pray for you as a reader of this book, that you will go out into the world and be the best you that you can be. That you will be the best representative of Christ that you can be, and that you can be the be representative of your culture and background that you be! Hallelujah!

Conclusion

My hope throughout this book hasn't been to offer a complete explanation of all of the concepts that I have discussed. If I'd have gone into the amount of depth into which I researched, this book would have been three or four times as thick. If I'd have used the technical terms found in my research, or 'proper' English, I would have missed the reason for writing the book – to reach out to my own culture and class with a radical, and yet biblical, way of living. However, it is my aim to encourage working-class people to put their thoughts into media and politics. It is my desire to see working-class ethics, aspirations, and concepts in academia. It is for this reason that I have gone out my way to include my research in an academic manner. If we are to have a real impact on this world we will need to break into every aspect of the world. If we want more rights in the workplace, we will need to win them in a political forum. If we want our aspirations to be accepted as valid in utilitarian society, then we will need to learn how to express them in the right manner. This book is my first attempt of many, with any luck and a bit of will power, to bring a working-class expression of life and thinking into the land of media and academia. It is my hope that college students would use this research, and my own experience, to further the cause for a chav spirituality. It is my dream that chav churches would begin to pop-up all over this nation as missionaries begin to read this book and learn how to speak and think chav. It is my goal to make sure that no single-parent, or chav-nan, has to walk for three miles or catch two buses on a Sunday morning to find a relevant and Spirit-filled church, where they feel at home and people don't try to 'transform' them into the likeness of their middle-class pastor. It makes my heart beat faster and stronger to know that you could be the person to start to the ball rolling on your estate.

Amen!

Bibliography

Books

Anderson A. *An Introduction To Pentecostalism: Global Charismatic Christianity*, Cambridge: Cambridge University Press, 2004.

Baildam J. D. *Paradisal Love: Johann Gottfried Herder and the Song of Songs*, Sheffield: Sheffield Academic Press, 1999.

Bennington J. *Culture, Class & Christian Beliefs*, London: Scripture Union, 1973.

Berger A. A. *Blind Men And Elephants: Perspectives on humor*, New Brunswick: Transaction Publishers, 1995.

Bok L. *The Little Book of Chavs*, Crombie: Jardine Publishing Limited, 2004.

Browne K. *Introducing Sociology For AS Level*, Oxford: Polity Press, 2006.

Buckingham M. & Clifton D. O. *Now, Discover Your Strengths: How to develop your talents and those of the people you manage*, London: Pocket Books, 2004.

Campbell R. & Campbell A. *Blood and Fire*, London: Arrow Books LTD, 2006.

Chester T. *Unreached: Growing churches in working-class and deprived areas*, Nottingham: Inter-Varsity Press, 2012.

Evans E. *The Welsh Revival Of 1904*, South Wales: Evangelical Press Of Wales, 1969.

Gascoigne P. & Davies H. *Gazza: My story*, London: Headline Book Publishing, 2004.

Gerrard P. *The Guv'nor: A celebration*, London: Blake Publishing Ltd, 2001.

Hathaway M. R. 'The Elim Pentecostal Church: Origins, development, and distinctives', K. Warrington (eds.) *Pentecostal Perspectives*, Carlisle: Paternoster Press, 1998.

Hattersly R. *John Wesley: A brand from the burning*, London: Time Warner Books UK, 2002.

Jones O. *Chavs: The demonization of the working class*, London: Verso, 2011.

Joslin R. *Urban Harvest: Biblical perspectives on Christian mission in the inner cities*, Welwyn: Evangelical Press, 1982.

Kay W. K. *Pentecostals in Britain*, Cumbria: Paternoster Press, 2000.

Kay W. *Pentecostalism: A very short introduction*, Oxford, Oxford University Press, 2011.

Kimball D. *The Emerging Church: Vintage Christianity for new generations*, Grand Rapids: Zondervan, 2003.

Lewis C. S. *A Grief Observed*, London: Faber & Faber Ltd, 1961.

Marjoribanks K. *Family and School Capital: Towards a context theory of students' school outcomes*, Norwell: Kluwer Academic Publishers, 2002.

Morgan J. *Let The Healing Begin*, Eastbourne: David C Cook, 2007.

Payne R. K. *A Framework For Understanding Poverty*, Highlands: Aha! Process Inc., 1996.

Scanlon P. *The 15 Revolution: Go ahead inconvenience me*, Bradford: Abundant Life Publishing, 2009.

Schwarz C. A. *The 3 Colors of Ministry*, St. Charles: ChurchSmart Resources, 2001.

Schwartz G. *Sect Ideologies and Social Status*, Chicago: The University of Chicago Press, 1970.

Sheaff M. *Sociology And Health Care*, Milton Keynes: Open University Press, 2005.

Toulis N. *Believing Identity: Pentecostalism and the meditation of Jamaican ethnicity and gender in England*, Oxford: Berg, 1997.

Tournier P. *A Listening Ear*, London: Hodder & Stoughton, 1984.

Wallace M. & Spanner C. *Chav: A user's guide to Britain's new ruling class*, London: Bantam Books, 2004.

Warrington K. *Pentecostal Theology: A theology of encounter*, London: T & T Clark, 2008.

Weitz R. *The Sociology Of Health, Illness, and Health Care*, Belmont: Cengage Learning, Inc., 2012.

Wilson B. R. *Sects and Society: the sociology of three religious groups in Britain*, London: William Heinemann LTD, 1961.

Wilson J. *Wigglesworth: the complete story*, Milton Keynes: Authentic Media, 2002.

Journals

Hathaway W. G. (ed.) "*Marvels of Healing*," The Elim Evangel, Vol xii Nos. 51 & 52 (1931), 28-29.

Haylett C. "'This is about us, this is our film!': Personal and popular discourses of 'Underclass'," *in Cultural Studies And The Working Class*, ed. Sally R. Munt, London: Cassell, 2000, 69-81.

Nelson T. J. "At ease with our own kind: Worship practices and class segregation in American religion," in *Religion and Class in America: culture, history and politics*, eds. S. McCloud & W. A. Mirola, Leiden: Brill, 2008, 45-68.

Websites

BBC News Magazine, 'What is working class?', http://news.bbc.co.uk/1/hi/magazine/6295743.stm, accessed 14th May 2013.

Butler P. The Guardian, '*Jack Monroe: the face of modern poverty*', http://www.guardian.co.uk/society/2013/jul/23/jack-monroe-face-modern-poverty?CMP=twt_gu, accessed 25th July 2013.

Cambridge Dictionaries Online, '*Chav*', http://dictionary.cambridge.org/dictionary/british/chav, accessed 16th May 2013.

Ellen B. The Observer, '*You stay working class all your life, so be proud of it*,' http://www.guardian.co.uk/commentisfree/2012/feb/26/barbara-ellen-your-class-stays-with-you, accessed 24th May 2013.

Fox K. The Telegraph, '*Everybody's talking about etiquette, but what we're really interested in is class,*' http://www.telegraph.co.uk/comment/personal-view/3618904/Everybodys-talking-about-etiquette-but-what-were-really-interested-in-is-class.html, accessed 23rd May 2013.

Lucas S. Victoria and Albert Museum, '*Close Encounters of the Art Kind: The old in out (saggy version),*' http://www.vam.ac.uk/content/articles/c/close-encounter-the-old-in-out-saggy-version-sarah-lucas/, accessed 25th May 2013.

Meaning that family bonds are stronger than any bonds with outsiders; The Phrase Finder, '*Blood is thicker than water,*' http://www.phrases.org.uk/meanings/67600.html, accessed 20th May 2013.

Movie Mistakes, '*Blackadder (1986),*' http://www.moviemistakes.com/tv3217/quotes/page2, accessed 27th May 2013.

Smith R. & Womack R. The Telegraph, '*Middle class are biggest abusers of alcohol*', http://www.telegraph.co.uk/news/uknews/1566292/Middle-class-are-biggest-abusers-of-alcohol.html, accessed 17th May 2013.

The Telegraph, '*Thalidomide: the timeline of scandal,*' http://www.telegraph.co.uk/health/healthnews/9513903/Thalidomide-timeline-of-a-scandal.html, accessed 21st May 2013.

UB40: The Official Site, '*The History: Introduction,*' http://www.ub40.co.uk/introduction.html, accessed 19th May 2013.

Lightning Source UK Ltd.
Milton Keynes UK
UKOW06f0606030917
308455UK00001B/1/P